Mother Tongue, Father Time

Mother Tongue, Father Time

A Decade of Linguistic Revolt

ALETTE OLIN HILL

INDIANA UNIVERSITY PRESS
Bloomington and Indianpolis

© 1986 by Alette Olin Hill

Manufactured in the United States of America

Library of Congress Cataloging-in Publication Data

Hill, Alette Olin, 1933-
Mother tongue, father time.

Bibliography: p.
Includes index.
1. Language and languages—Sex differences.
2. Sexism in language. I. Title.
P120.S48H54   1986   401'.9   85–45582
ISBN O–253–33879–4
ISBN O–253–20389–9 (pbk.)

1   2   3   4   5   90   89   87   86

For Boyd, Buck, and Michael,
*without whose relentless chauvinism
this book might not have been written*

That is the modern experience, the clash between a first and a second reality, between which no bridge exists, and no common language, although all the individual words that make up the two languages are common to each.

—Heimito von Doderer, *The Demons*

CONTENTS

Acknowledgments

I should like to thank Professors Lee Chambers-Schiller and Patricia Limerick of the Department of History, University of Colorado at Boulder, and Professor Marcia Westkott, Department of Sociology, University of Colorado at Colorado Springs, for suggestions about editors and publishers. I should also like to thank Professor Megan McClard, Department of English, and Dr. Gwen Thomas, Assistant Vice President for Institutional Advancement, Metropolitan State College, Denver. Shirley Sims, Coordinator of Women's Services at Metropolitan State College, coerced me in her ladylike way into giving a talk ("Women, Language, and Power"), which forced me to condense the salient points of my manuscript and try out my ideas on a lively audience.

I acknowledge with gratitude the opinions of my longtime friend Pat Huggins Moore, Director of Compliance, Office of Fair Housing & Equal Opportunity, Region VIII of HUD. She urged me to drop my romance-writing endeavors in favor of more scholarly and academic pursuits, and I must agree that her logic was impeccable. It is ironical that the strongest support I have ever received for anything I have written came from a group of romance writers, whose names deserve to be listed because of their encouragement, wit, and expert criticism: Maggie Osborne, Linda Wager, Karen Conley, Mary Ellen Johnson, Diane Hoover, Roberta Kahn, Sandy Schlut, Carol Caverly, Terry Coke-Kerr, Sandy Lamb, Pat Agnew, and Judy Ellis.

For inspiration over the past twelve years, I owe an enormous debt of gratitude to Professor Barbara Nieweg Blansett, who launched the Women's Studies program at Metropolitan State College in 1972 and has steered it through the rocky shoals of both radical and conservative waters with equal success. Without her remarkable intelligence and unfailing sense of humor I would never have persevered in a discipline that elicits so little enthusiasm from the Establishment.

Finally, *mange tusen takk* to Ann Underwood, who, while typing the manuscript, caught a flagrant error of interpretation in my argument.

Introduction

The title *Mother Tongue, Father Time* suggests two related ideas: (1) the issue of sexism embedded in language and (2) the fact that language changes over time. The title also raises the question: Why is our native language called "Mother" whereas Time is called "Father"? One easy answer to the first is that most infants learn to speak from their mother and therefore say "Mama" before "Papa" or "Dada." Thus, "Mother Tongue" is named for the person from whom we pick up our first or native language. "Father Time," on the other hand, has a more mysterious and perhaps sinister history. According to art historian Erwin Panofsky, Father Time and Death share a joint career in the history of ideas, from classical antiquity to the cartoon trademark for the Bowery Savings Bank.[1]

Father Time, depicted as an ancient bearded man holding a scythe, merges easily with Death the Grim Reaper, whose phantom face is shrouded by a hood or revealed as a skull. Panofsky never asks the question: Why should Time/Death be embodied in male form? On every December 31st, we see Father Time in his traditional garb, to be replaced on January first by the image of a newborn babe. Father Time gives birth? Well, not exactly. This is but one instance of the unaccountable absence of the female at the scene of the action (generic birthing?).

It is noteworthy that Mother Tongue, meaning native language, belongs to human anatomy, whereas Father Time cannot be pinned down to a part of the body. Time is a more abstract concept than speech, an invention of Thinkers (traditionally males). Everyone knows what a tongue is, and it's probably female because women supposedly talk more than men, a folktale that has been exploded in the last decade. Perhaps in a patriarchal society Time/Death is male because a man (e.g., the *paterfamilias* of Roman society) had the right of life and death over his family. Given such legal and psychological power, it is only fitting that Time be a man.

The earth, ships, and tongues are female. Freud would have understood why. Earth is a womb for us; ships are womb-shaped; tongues are phallic, but that's the usual proportion of congruence in Freudian analysis. One wonders how Freud, after talking to women for decades, could utter with Job-like anguish, "What do women want?" After all of his arduous work, this answer eluded him. Women remained a riddle, obstinately refusing to yield up their innermost secrets.

Or maybe they didn't. Recent scholarship suggests that Freud's early patients who reported incest were telling the truth, even though Freud changed his mind and decided that they were all fantasizing. He referred to his daughter Anna as "my only son," though he fathered three male children. This metaphor demonstrates that he attributed intellectual activity and carrying on the family business to males only.

One must admit that Freud's analysis of men could be as cockeyed as those of women: his only thoroughly documented case, the so-called "Wolf-Man," defies comprehension.[2] Part One tells of the patient's pitiable life as a Russian émigré in Vienna (following loss of the family palace and wealth, preceded by the suicide of his only sister and closest friend, and other suicides in the immediate family) told in the Wolf-Man's own words. Part Two is Freud's analysis of the origins of the Wolf-Man's problems: they were not to be found in the tragedies of his early life but rather in the fact that at the age of eighteen months or so he witnessed his parents having sex in the afternoon. There is nothing in Part One that Freud can use to prove his theory; he deduces it from the Wolf-Man's dreams, none of which involved his parents in the act of copulation.

Yet Freud's so-called "scientific" approach continues to be defended. Erich Fromm admitted that the master's view of women was "grotesque," yet he offered Freud's last session with "Dora" as an example of his "objective attitude."[3] From Dora's statement that she had decided to stop coming and had made that decision a fortnight earlier, Freud replies, "'That sounds just like a maidservant or a governess—a fortnight's warning.'" Fromm points out that Freud did not get angry with Dora; rather, he "spent the rest of the session analyzing what this acting out of the role of a maidservant really meant."[4] To me this is worse than leading the witness, for it was Freud who both suggested the parallel with a maidservant and then forced the patient to discuss her "acting out" of the maidservant role. In short, Dora was verbally degraded for her assertion that she intended to stop coming to the doctor. Fromm's labeling of this incident as scientific and objective is as ludicrous as Freud's own verbal gymnastics to get Dora where he wanted her—in a malleable position.

Freud's treatment consisted in verbal activity—language was his scalpel—but his tortuous explanations of the roots of neurotic symptoms are difficult for feminists to accept because of his insistence that "Anatomy is destiny" and his equation of female anatomy with the womb. Women also have arms, legs, and—most controversial of all— tongues, for it is the tongue that provides evidence for the mind. Admittedly, the tongue is useful for eating; it can also be used in kissing and other erotic activities; but its most wondrous capacity and source of creativity is its role in the act of speech.

An assumption of this book is that woman's most powerful weapon is indeed her tongue—not her womb, her legs, her bust, or her face. Linguists have been arguing for the last decade or so about the way women speak: (1) They talk differently from men and should continue to do so; (2) Their different manner of speech dooms them to perpetual servitude, and they should emulate men if they want to improve their lot; (3) Changing one's speech won't change one's condition; and (4) One cannot revolutionize a language at will, so why worry about it?

What I have found among the avant garde (men as well as women and not all of them linguists) are suggestions as to how to create an androgynous language. Textbooks are scrutinized for rampant sexism. Publishers have issued guidelines on how to write gender-free prose. Authors are consequently caught between the Scylla of sexism and the Charybdis of style, two female monsters. Perhaps a truly androgynous language will emerge in time, but before embracing those who would do away with our ancient pronouns *he* and *she* or replace *history* with *herstory*, we should review what has actually happened to our language during the years 1975–84, whether it's good or bad, and finally whether we can and should do anything about it.[5]

The following essays do not cover the entire history of gender-related language changes in American English during the decade in question. Rather, they highlight certain areas that proved useful to me. I inaugurated a course called "Women and Language" at Metropolitan State College in Denver in the fall semester of 1974, and have

continued to teach this course during the intervening years. My initial
sortie into the field proved a difficult campaign, since it was B. L.
(Before Lakoff—*Language and Woman's Place* was published in 1975).
After 1974, books and articles on "women's language" and "sexist language" began to appear in quantity. I define "women's language" as
the language spoken *by* women and "sexist language" as the language
spoken *to* and *about* women (speaker's sex is irrelevant) if that language degrades, disparages, or otherwise criticizes women. I covered
both "women's language" and "sexist language" in my course, explaining as best I could the linguistic jargon in the sources to students
not trained in the discipline.

At the same time, I was also teaching an introductory course in
Women's Studies called "Woman in Transition." It bothered me that
so few of the books sent to me by eager publishers contained a section
on language. Only the earliest anthology—Vivian Gornick and Barbara K. Moran's *Woman in Sexist Society: Studies in Power and Powerlessness* (New York: Basis Books, 1971)—dealt with language explicitly
(Christine Pierce, "Natural Law Language and Women" and Ethel
Strainchamps, "Our Sexist Language"). Sheila Ruth, a philosopher,
did not include a single selection by a linguist in *Issues in Feminism: A
First Course in Women's Studies* (Boston: Houghton Mifflin, 1980). Since
philosophy depends almost entirely upon language for its exposition
and development, Ruth's omission seemed strange to me. I had the
same impression when I adopted *Women's Realities, Women's Choices* by
the Hunter College Women's Studies Collective (New York: Oxford
University Press, 1983). The authors agonize over how to treat pronouns in their preface, but they have no significant portion of the
book devoted to language. Perhaps this lacuna in an otherwise splen-
did text can be attributed to the absence of a linguist from the Collective.

The paucity of information on the linguistic aspects of women's
plight contained in introductory texts and the technical complexity
of the material in books for courses on "Women and Language"
prompted me to write the following essays. They contain a cross section of the arguments about women and language since 1975, yet they
assume no training in linguistics on the part of the reader. This book
is designed to be accessible to anyone interested in "women's language," "sexist language," and the arguments about each that have
emerged since 1975. I have not confined myself to publications by linguists and other scholars whose primary concern is language analysis

but have used a wide range of sources including quotations from soft-core popular culture.

For the reader who wants to explore anything mentioned in the following pages in greater depth, I recommend *Language, Gender and Society,* edited by Barrie Thorne, Cheris Kramarae, and Nancy Henley (Rowley, Mass.: Newbury House, 1983). The section entitled "Sex Similarities and Differences in Language, Speech, and Nonverbal Communication: An Annotated Bibliography" (pp. 151–331) is a gold mine of information, subdivided into many categories and summarized by the editors in a most succinct fashion.

A guide through the maze of linguistic research that erupted around 1975 can be found in Cheris Kramarae, *Women and Men Speaking: Frameworks for Analysis* (Rowley, Mass.: Newbury House, 1981). Kramarae's four approaches are the "Muted Group," "Reconstructed Psychoanalysis," "Speech Styles," and "Strategy" frameworks, and they are just as valuable as heuristic devices for material published since 1981 as for what appeared before. Kramarae's remarkable ability to make plain what is obscure in the sources is amply demonstrated in the section on "Reconstructed Psychoanalysis" (chapters 4 and 5), most notably in her lucid interpretation of the work of the difficult French analyst Jacques Lacan. This book is virtually indispensable for putting masses of disparate research into coherent perspectives.

What follows is a Cook's tour of Mt. St. Helens after the first eruption. The question that perplexes me most is why it took so long for the mountain to explode. If women speak differently from men and if men have been hurling abuse at women or interrupting and silencing them since the dawn of recorded history, why was the topic (like the mountain) so seemingly lifeless, so still, so innocuous? To be sure, there were rumblings and angry sounds before the Big Bang, but these were not perceived as significant. Hints can be found in Dale Spender, *Women of Ideas and What Men Have Done to Them: From Aphra Behn to Adrienne Rich* (London: Ark Paperbacks, 1983). In the introduction to Part 1, "Why Didn't I Know?," the author tells us that in the late 1960s she was trying "to find out whether other women felt and thought as I did in a male-dominated society." She found that, indeed, cohorts existed, and they began to talk at length about their personal misgivings:

> We realised that the problems we faced, and the discrepancies we encountered between what we were supposed to be and feel and what we

were and felt in our own terms, were not idiosyncratic in origin, nor a
product of individual deficiency as many of us had believed. Looking
back, I know what we thought when we found that there was nothing
'wrong' with ourselves that we had discovered something 'new' (which in
a sense, we had) and we experienced a feeling of elation that goes with
finding a more meaningful and positive way of viewing the world and
ourselves.[6]

Spender then turned to the past to see if other women had felt the
way she did. She found many, and she traced the careers of these
women as far back as the seventeenth century. The pattern of harass-
ment, humiliation, and outright suppression of women's voices was
so clear that Spender concluded there had doubtless been women
throughout the ages who must have rebelled against men's evaluation
of them as subordinates if not slaves.

By the mid-seventies there were many female voices being raised
against the tyranny of patriarchal Loud Mouths. Language itself was
being examined as both an instrument of oppression and as a possible
tool of liberation. What I find most striking about the linguistic explo-
sion of the 70's and early 80's is the closing of ranks by men who defended their inalienable right to manage the controversy. One of the
stock rebuttals to women who investigated language for its power
over their lives was to trivialize the discussion. ("Now, now, my dear,
don't get so worked up. Besides, you don't know what you're talking
about.")

When this book was accepted for publication and I happened to
mention this fact to a scholar at a reception on the Boulder campus,
he launched into a tirade against the stupidities of feminist language
changes ("girlcott" for "boycott," etc.) "But I would never argue for
that," I replied, and after three more sallies by the learned gentleman
against the content of my book (which he hadn't allowed me to discuss), I retreated into silence. He had never once asked me about my
essays; he merely cowed me into submission by ranting and raving
against asinine females. I was about to retreat physically when his
wife, seeing her husband becoming red-faced and hot under the collar, led him away to a cooler part of the room. Perhaps I am now on
his Vipers Hit List, even though I did nothing to deserve it except to
announce the title of the book. If his only regular exercise were jumping to conclusions, I would dismiss it, but he is known for his objectiv-
ity, his intellectual prowess, and his interest in linguistics. I was

evidently perceived as "part of the problem," as Freud so smartly said to the women in the audience at a lecture he presented in London in 1931. In fact, Freud said, "Your *are* the problem," a good way to shut up any wayward feminists in the crowd. I simply won't shut up any more just because I have been given the brush-off. The topic is too interesting and too important for me to retreat into silence.

Mother Tongue, Father Time

1

Women's Language

In 1975, Robin Lakoff, associate professor of linguistics at Berkeley, published a small paperback called *Language and Woman's Place*.[1] The cover design by Catherine Hopkins shows a woman's face with a band-aid covering her mouth; her large expressive eyes look troubled. The message is clear: women have been gagged. Why can't this distressed lady simply rip off the bandaid? one might ask. She can and she has in real life. Lakoff does not argue that women have been forced into to-tal silence: they have been socialized into certain speech patterns. These patterns correlate with women's subordinate position in soci-ety ("woman's place").

Language and Woman's Place set off a debate in the linguistic commu-nity and beyond. The general public treated it as a loose cannon on the deck, endangering the lives of "ladies" or threatening to polarize the sexes still further by suggesting that women speak a different lan-guage from that of men. Scholars reacted to her assertions with skep-ticism, disbelief, and charges of being "unscientific." Why? Her style is anything but strident, and her introductory remarks modest. Admit-ting that she has based her conclusions on data "gathered mainly by introspection," making use of "intuitions" in analyzing her own speech and that of her acquaintances as well as the media, she con-cludes: "I present what follows less as the final word on the subject of sexism in language—anything but that!—than as a goad to further re-search."[2] In her stated intent she has been wildly successful.

1

Penelope Brown was one of the few who grasped the pioneering nature of *Language and Woman's Place:*

> This is a highly idiosyncratic and provocative book, a first attempt by a linguist to characterize the stylistic features of women's speech in English and to account for these features by grounding them in social factors: the position of women in American society. It is admittedly a preliminary analysis, intended to provoke more detailed research into this question and not to pose as the last word on the subject.[3]

Others were not so complimentary. Barrie Thorne puzzled over "the empirical status of her assertions about sex differences in speaking patterns."[4] Eleanor Kuykendall, a philosopher and one of the few humanists to review the book, criticized it on internal grounds: "Robin Lakoff . . . vacillates between two theoretical conceptions of language."[5] In Kuykendall's opinion, Lakoff's failure to distinguish between two forms of linguistic competence "amounts to creating another double bind about what knowledge of language is."[6]

Francine Wattman Frank exhibited extreme skepticism:

> Do women in this country show a preference for tag questions, compound requests, passives, hedges, and intensifiers? If so, is this true of all women in all situations? And what is the explanation for such behavior? Lakoff points to women's use of such forms as indications of the nonassertive, inferior, "lady-like" role ascribed to them in our culture.[7]

She concluded that perceptions about male/female language differences follow prevalent stereotypes, but as for *reality,* "A search for empirical support for claims about syntactic differences in the language of women and men reveals that there are very few studies in print which attempt to document these alleged differences."[8] Frank continues: "The few studies which do attempt some documentation of the differences seems [sic] to have been inspired by *indignation* over the absence of empirical evidence in Lakoff's 1973 article."[9] The few articles that were available to Frank in 1978 were largely unsatisfactory: either the results were contradictory or the sample was too restricted or both. Unfortunately, this is still true today. In spite of the empirical work that has been done, it is impossible to conclude with any confidence that Lakoff's nine features are the norm for most women in most situations.

It is instructive to peruse the literature by "indignant" scholars in various fields.[10] Sometimes their samples are as small as five dyads (a total of ten people); sometimes their sample is large enough to prove something, but the results are unconvincing. One can be swept away by the precautions taken by the researchers, dazzled by the care with which they set up their experiments, and yet question their findings, for laboratory or classroom exercises will not necessarily yield a sample of language that is a reliable gauge of how people really talk when unmonitored. Lakoff covered her bets when she said that she did not pretend that her book represented the ways in which all American women speak; she even admitted that perhaps no one individual woman in the U.S. spoke as she had indicated. Her own self-description of her work is still the best measure of her intent: she was presenting what she herself had observed in unguarded conversations, not in the laboratory.

Here is the Catch 22 of linguistic field work: when one announces to a group of people that their language is being studied, they invariably become self-conscious. Reports of "spies" are therefore useful. One such spy is Dale Spender, a feminist whose training is in history and literature, but who has also written with great acumen about language. In this case she was also spying on herself, for after attending a conference on sexism and education in London, she replayed the tape of the workshop. The group was composed of thirty-two women and only five men, yet the men dominated the discussion. Now, although the interruption of women by men is not one of Lakoff's nine traits, her assessment of women's language as a nonassertive, always "polite," idiom lends itself to the question of how much and how well women tolerate interruption. Spender was aware of the scholarship on interruption (research undertaken by those who would test the stereotype that women talk *more* than men). Some authors had asserted that men interrupt women far more than women interrupt men. Some were not so convinced and ultimately defined what constituted a bona fide interruption: it should be construed as a break into someone else's conversation for the purpose of taking over, for silencing the other person.

Here is what Spender found when she replayed her tape:

Whereas many females wanted to discuss their own experience of sexism, the men wanted to talk in more general and 'abstract' terms. Women wanted to talk about what happened to them while, generally speaking, the men wanted to talk about sexism in the curriculum and sexism 'in the system'. One of the most noticeable features of this discussion—which I wasn't aware of at the time—was that it was men who determined what the topic would be. They did the interrupting and they insisted that the discussion get back to the point: *their* point.[11]

One does not have to be at an academic meeting to appreciate the reality of what Spender describes. If men listen to women at all, they often behave as if they have an innate prerogative to direct the conversation, whereas women, if left to their own devices, will supposedly "wander off the topic." Spender perceived that "wandering off the topic" *was* the topic: the men would not allow the women to run a workshop according to their own perception of what was important. Women's approach was "wrong" by definition. One senses here a powerful paternal drive; the males felt that they had to redirect the females as if they were hyperactive children. Spender's analysis of this workshop is as follows:

> There is no doubt in my mind that in this context at least (and I do not think it was an atypical one) it was the five males and not the thirty-two females who were defining the parameters of the talk. I suspect that neither the women nor the men were conscious of this. There was no overt hostility displayed towards the females who 'strayed from the point', but considerable pressure was exerted by the males—and accepted without comment by the females—to confine the discussion to the male definition of the topic. . . . No male gave any indication that he thought the female perspective was valid and I would say that the males were made 'uncomfortable' by the women's wish to talk about their personal experience of sexism in education.[12]

If five men can dominate thirty–two women in a workshop about sexism and education, and this experience can be verified by the reader, then we might conclude that one individual's experience (Spender's) proves something about inter-sex conversations among presumptive "peers." Since Spender's observations corroborate my own during countless meetings and conferences, I conclude that her "intuitive" leap to interpretation is justified. Notice that the women at the workshop were no more privy to the hidden agenda than were the men. Only by post-game replay via tape was Spender able to analyze what really happened at the conference.

Spender's analysis of interruption and dominance at a workshop seems solid and believable. She generalizes to some extent from the conference she attended to other situations where male interference or bossiness is probably to be found ("and I do not think it was an atypical one"). The difference between Spender and Lakoff is that Spender made a tape of a meeting and then subjected it to scrutiny. Lakoff made no tapes; rather, she replayed those in her head, drawing upon her memory alone. Another difference between these two authors is in their isolation of specific language traits: Lakoff listed nine major features of "women's language," whereas Spender merely said that the thirty–two women at the conference endured interruption and followed male direction, without offering any precise syntactic or intonational guide as to how this was accomplished. Both authors are impressionistic, but only one (Lakoff) supplied a bill of particulars, each of which could be challenged by skeptics.

Although the furor has subsided, references to Lakoff still abound in articles and books on the subject of language and women (including both how women speak and how they are spoken to and about). What is not generally found in the literature about her book are the following: (1) acceptance of her claims as hypothetical, (2) recognition of her wit and subtlety, and (3) an account of her personal metamorphosis from ivory-tower classicist to contemporary sociolinguist.

It is instructive to peruse her first book, *Abstract Syntax and Latin Complementation*, a revision of her doctoral dissertation (Harvard 1967) published by M.I.T. Press as "Research Monograph No. 49" in 1968. Even if you know Latin and are familiar with the principles of transformational generative grammar, you may find this book challenging, but you will not find it threatening. It is totally apolitical; the subject of whether the ancient Romans—male and female—used different kinds of Latin is not even broached. How appropriate to find at the end of the Acknowledgment:

> I should also like to thank my husband, George Lakoff, for aid and comfort above and beyond the vows of matrimony. His suggestions and comments have directly shaped this thesis; his development of transformational theory is what makes such a work possible. He has lived for a year on hamburgers and TV dinners, suffering along with me the day-to-day crises of thesis writing. To him, a double portion of Peking Duck.[13]

This sounds suspiciously defensive today. Why didn't George do the cooking while his wife was working on her dissertation? I know the answer because I was working on my own dissertation at the time, and on an equally recondite topic ("Sievers-Edgerton's Law and the Indo-European Semivowels in Greek"). I too made a lot of hamburgers and other fast food, although TV dinners were not allowed (Southerners as husbands involve a culinary digression that will not be explored here).

In *Language and Woman's Place* we find a startling contrast to Lakoff's apologia seven years earlier: the dedication reads "For ANDY whose generation will, I hope, have transcended these issues by the time it can read this book." Lakoff's consciousness has obviously been raised, and her topic now confronts the emotionally charged situation of women's position (linguistic and otherwise) in modern-day America. I too made a startling transition between 1969 and 1974 from teacher of Sanskrit and Indo-European linguistics to teacher of Women and Language—from theoretical linguistics, that is, to sociolinguistics. Millions of women altered their *Weltanschauung* between the late 60's and the mid-70's, the transition from observer to participant taking various outward forms.

Lakoff was not the first scholar to explore the subject of how women speak. Mary Ritchie Key's *Male/Female Language* appeared in the same year as *Language and Woman's Place,* and so did the interdisciplinary collection of articles edited by Barrie Thorne and Nancy Henley, *Language and Sex: Difference and Dominance.*[14] The latter contains the following statement on the back cover:

> *Language and Sex* identifies fascinating new theoretical leads for both linguists and researchers in women's studies. It seems destined to be one of those seminal books which will give rise to many other works as students and scholars explore the paths pointed out by Thorne and Henley.

Despite its excellence (including an elaborate annotated bibliography), Lakoff's *Language and Woman's Place* seems to have been more "seminal" in the intervening decade. Her book *goaded* others into irritation.

One of the reasons may be that her approach ran counter to the training of other scholars, most of whom are in the social sciences. Lakoff did not use the correct "code" for social scientists (specialized vocabulary and a format that often entails quantification, statistical formulae, and illustrative charts).* Nor does she make use of her background in transformational generative grammar, a branch of lin-

---

*In recent years the science model has been attacked by some social scientists who have turned instead to the humanities for inspiration. See "Questioning the Science in Social Science, Scholars Signal a 'Turn to Interpretation,' " *The Chronicle of Higher Education,* June 26, 1985, pp. 5–6.

guistics that can be compared to the "new math" of the field. Though "applied" in that actual utterances are used in some of its exposition, transformational generative grammar works from a theoretical base that is abstract, more concerned with "competence" than with "performance."[15] Since Lakoff's focus in *Language and Woman's Place* is linguistic performance and its social origins and implications, transformational generative grammar (the theoretical basis of her dissertation) has little utility here.

The incompatibility of Lakoff's "introspective-intuitive" analysis with the analyses engendered by social scientists can be found in her book on pages 58–59 where she defends herself against Cheris Kramer. Kramer had evidently read Lakoff in article form (*Language in Society,* 1973), for she comments briefly on some of Lakoff's "women's language" traits (the tag question, statements with question intonation, and "feminine" adjectives) in an article called "Folk-linguistics: Wishy-Washy Mommy Talk."[16] Her study centers on stereotypes of women's speech and the folklore surrounding these stereotypes, whereas Lakoff focuses on how women actually talk. Kramer used cartoons from *The New Yorker* but submitted only the captions to a test group (twenty-five male and twenty-five female students) to see if they could identify the speech as belonging to men or women. "For most of the 49 captions, there was a clear consensus (at least sixty-six percent agreement) that the speaker in the cartoon was of a particular sex."[17].

In her book, Lakoff counters, "Cartoon captions, minus the cartoons of course, which have . . . been used as a testing device, will . . . produce suspect results, because they are not part of a connected dialogue and because they are contextless."[18] She seems momentarily to have lost sight of the fact that Kramer was testing for stereotypes, not for actual speech. Where Lakoff introduces Kramer's statement that women do not necessarily speak as folklore suggests, she objects to Kramer's use of questionnaires and interviews to elicit information (both of which are social science tools, though Lakoff does not label them as such).[19]

It is an axiom of linguistics that when an investigator focuses an informant's attention upon his or her language, the informant becomes self-conscious and invariably stops speaking "naturally." If the informant is indeed speaking naturally, a layperson is not able to analyze this parlance. "Very often," writes Lakoff, "people simply aren't aware of what they say; it takes a trained linguist to have the 'ear' for that."[20] This appears to be an attack against Kramer, then instructor (now professor) of speech communication at the University of Illinois. Speech communication and linguistics are distinct fields though they may deal with the same subject matter. Thus, Kramer's tools and her ability to analyze the real thing when she hears it are both called into question.

Lakoff's remarks can be seen as a defense of her argument that "women's language" exists—something that Kramer denied. "Women's language" existed only as a stereotype for Kramer, yet to test this hypothesis she had to assess women's real language. From questionnaires and interviews, she concluded that women do not speak a separate language, but she did not dismiss as trivial the *belief* that "women's language" exists. "Beliefs about sex-related language differences may be as important as the actual differences. As long as women play a subordinate role, their speech will be stereotyped as separate and unequal."[21]

Lakoff's position is that women's *actual* language demonstrates and reinforces their subordinate role in society, but she does not overlook the power of stereotypes—an idea that follows immediately after her rebuttal of Kramer and appears to be an expansion of Kramer's thesis:

> . . . a stereotypical image may be far more influential than a (mere) statistical correlation. Let's say, for the sake of argument, that *no* real female person in the United States actually speaks any form or dialect of women's language. Yet there are innumerable women we see on television, who whether we like it or not form role models for young girls. Maybe Edith Bunker is not presented as a wholly believable figure, but certainly she is presented as a conceivable female type, one that someone might eventually aspire to fit into. Edith Bunker is obviously an extreme case, but almost every woman you see in the media has many traits of women's language built into her speech. And these stereotypical women, I fear, have great influence over the young.[22]

On this point, at least—the existence and power of linguistic stereotypes—Lakoff and Kramer are in accord.

In Part II, "Why Women Are Ladies," Lakoff answers anonymous critics who seem to have heard rather than to have read her ideas. These people to whom she presented her findings accepted the fact that nonparallel constructions occurred in the language, but did not perceive that these constructions demonstrated inequity between the sexes or that anything need be done to banish or equalize them.

Examples of nonparallel usages can be found in Part I of *Language and Woman's Place.* In earlier times a pair of words might have been simple male/female equivalents as "bull/cow" are today. Take "master/mistress," but compare the following sentences:

(18) *(a)* He is a master of the intricacies of academic politics.
    (b) *She is a mistress . . . *(LAWP,* p. 28)*

Obviously "master" and "mistress" are no longer equivalent. In another example Lakoff demonstrates that one and the same word has different connotations depending on whether it is applied to a man or a woman:

(21) *(a)* He's a professional.
    (b) She's a professional. *(LAWP,* p. 30)

Supposedly *(a)* would be construed as a doctor or lawyer; *(b)* as a prostitute.

Audiences did not take kindly to such information. "People very often feel affronted at my criticisms—this is true of both men and women—because they have been taught that the discrepancies actually favor women, and here I am trying to change them; I am striking a blow against womankind and maybe even mankind, since it benefits women and everyone else to have these distinctions."[23]

She goes on to say that the argument centers on the notion of "politeness" and hinges on the traditional view of women as "the preservers of morality and civility. . . . " Women's language (e.g., no slang or swearing) distinguishes it from the coarse, vulgar language of men; accordingly, women are typically exalted rather than denigrated by the speech used to and about them. Thus, Lakoff writes, her theory that discrepancies should be eliminated is perceived as "denigrating and degrading" to women.[24] Lakoff counters that a woman who is content to be a "lady" ("arbiter of morality, judge of manners") has accepted a status as less than a human being. The language used by and about "ladies" is actually damaging—the reverse of what we have been taught to believe. Her strong commitment to what has now become a cornerstone of feminism is illustrated in her personal credo: "if some women want to be arbiters of morality, that's fine with me; but I don't like the idea that, because I came into the world with two X chromosomes, I have no choice but to be an arbiter of morality, and will automatically be treated as though I were."[25]

*The asterisk at the beginning of *(b)* denotes an ungrammatical sentence, that is, one that the native speaker will reject as incorrect or unidiomatic.

The concept of "lady" goes far beyond a single word to a whole way of life. Concomitantly, the rules of politeness "are deleterious to society in general as well as to women in particular, and are not the innocent flattery they are thought of as being."[26] Before Lakoff can explore the rules of politeness, the contrast with men's and "neutral" language, and the reasons for sex-related discrepancies, she lists nine characteristics of women's language (overlapping to some extent with what she has already said in Part I but expanding and clarifying where necessary). In somewhat abbreviated form, women's language traits consist of the following:

(1) Words related to women's special interests—shades of color, sewing terms—that a man wouldn't ordinarily use because he does not know them.

(2) " 'Empty' adjectives like *divine, charming, cute. . . .* "

(3) "Question intonation where we might expect declaratives, for instance, tag questions ('It's so hot, isn't it?') and rising intonation in statement contexts ('What's your name, dear?' 'Mary Smith?')."

(4) Hedges ("well," "y'know," "kinda") . . . "words that convey the sense that the speaker is uncertain about what he (or she) is saying, and cannot vouch for the accuracy of the statement." Lakoff adds that hedges can be justified if they are used to spare someone's feelings, but used to excess "hedges, like question intonation, give the impression that the speaker lacks authority and doesn't know what he's talking about."

(5) The intensive "so" in place of a stronger and more precise adverb like "very." She characterizes "so" as a "weasel" word.

(6) Hypercorrect grammar. Girls are scolded for saying "ain't," whereas boys can get away with it (and other nonstandard forms). "Generally women are viewed as being the preservers of literacy and culture, at least in Middle America, where literacy and culture are viewed as being somewhat suspect in a male." This situation is reversed in societies in which men are the "guardians of culture."

(7) "Superpolite forms." This feature ties in with (6) but goes beyond it: "women are the experts of euphemisms; more positively, women are the repositories of tact . . . while men carelessly blurt out whatever they are thinking."

(8) "Women don't tell jokes"—an elaboration of (6) and (7). "It is axi-

omatic in middle-class American society that, first, women can't tell jokes—they are bound to ruin the punch line, they mix up the order of things. . . . Moreover, they don't 'get' jokes. In short, women have no sense of humor." One might also deduce from this axiom that women are incapable of sequential thought, that is, stupid.

(9) "Women speak in italics"—Lakoff's term for emphatic voice intonation. Though seemingly a sign of strong speech, "italic" speech is a ploy to gain the hearer's attention through vocal stress precisely because a woman is perceived as a weak person with little to say worth listening to.*

Repetition is used for the same purpose, though Lakoff does not include this trait in her list.[27]

These nine characteristics comprise the distilled data base from which Lakoff proceeds to make sociological conclusions. Girls are taught to speak this language in order to become "ladies," but the results are unrewarding. Having internalized these rules for feminine parlance, women find that they are not taken seriously. "If a woman learns and uses women's language, she is necessarily considered less than a real, full person—she's a bit of fluff."[28]

Lakoff asserts that woman is therefore damned if she does and damned if she doesn't—a paradox called the "double bind," that she attributes to Gregory Bateson.[29] Matina Horner had come to a parallel conclusion with regard to the educational attainments of bright women: the "motive to avoid success" is directly proportional to a fe-

---

*The fact that people with power need not speak in italics is illustrated in the following passage from *The Demons* by Heimito von Doderer. Prince Alfons Croix has invited Leonhard Kakabsa into a crowded cafe to discuss something urgent. The year is 1927.

In spite of the din of the café, the prince's speech effortlessly conquered its environment. That was the first thing Leonhard felt; he had a keen ear for such linguistic matters. The prince came through. Leonhard even had a rather exact idea why: the prince came through because he did not force his way, did not force himself upon his listener, was not in the least forceful. He merely made an experimental cast, without in the least disturbing his own balance. In fact, this maintenance of equilibrium while he spoke—so, for a second, it seemed to Leonhard—was in a way the principal aim of his speech, far more important than anything he actually communicated.

(*Die Dämonen*, 1956; trans. Richard and Clara Winston [New York: Alfred A. Knopf, 1961], p. 1102.)

male student's fear of loss of "femininity" engendered by success in the classroom: "A bright woman is caught in a double bind."[30] Though Horner used social science methodology, the test group to whom she administered the standard TAT achievement measures was considered too small and/or unrepresentative—"90 girls and 88 boys, all undergraduates at the University of Michigan."[31] Perhaps her statistical sample would have passed muster had she not followed the test with another assignment. She asked each student to tell a story based on the following sentence: *"After first-term finals, John (Anne) finds himself (herself) at the top of his (her) medical-school class."* The results were electrifying. The girls described Anne as "an acne-faced bookworm," "a *lonely* doctor," a drop-out who didn't want to be "number one," abnormal, guilt-ridden, on the brink of a nervous breakdown, a transfer to social work or nursing, and (most revealing of all) not a real person: "Anne is a *code name* for a nonexistent person created by a group of med. students. They take turns writing exams for Anne. . . ."

Horner quantified the results as follows: "Fifty-nine girls—over 65 percent—told stories that fell into one or another of the above categories. But only eight boys, fewer than 10 percent, showed evidence of the motive to avoid success. (These differences are significant at better than the .0005 level.)"[32] Horner used the correct social science code, but the students did not. They were not constrained by someone else's vocabulary on a multiple-choice test: they were asked to tell a story. Their vivid descriptions of Anne are revealing, particularly the one that refused to admit that Anne could possibly be first in the class but had to be an invention. A second story reflecting denial of the possibility of female superiority said that a boy in the class had done better than Anne though the statement given the student said clearly that Anne was "at the top."

Horner's findings on the "double bind" accord strikingly with Lakoff's remarks on women's language, for academic success means radically different social results between the sexes. Horner characterized most of the young men who took her test as "incipient Horatio Algers. They expressed unequivocal delight at John's success . . . and projected a grand and glorious future for him. *There was none of the hostility, bitterness and ambivalence that the girls felt for Anne.*"[33] Hostility is demonstrated in the first example in Horner's article: "Anne starts proclaiming her surprise and joy. Her fellow classmates are so disgusted with her behavior that they jump on her in a body and beat her. She is maimed for life."[34]

If these young women were caught in a double bind between their intellectual achievements and society's expectations of them as "marriage material," it is small wonder that they would also be caught in a linguistic bind—having to choose whether to talk like a "lady" or like a grownup. Admittedly Horner's test group was composed of college students, whereas Lakoff has no official test group whatsoever, but since she draws on personal encounters, one may conclude that the generalizations she makes about "women's language" must be derived to some extent from academe. From her slurs about Middle America it seems clear that the locutions she lists were gleaned from students and colleagues at a state university (quintessential Middle America) as well as from the media.

Resistance to Horner's "motive to avoid success" and Lakoff's "women's language" can be readily understood in the context of a supposedly egalitarian society.[35] The implications of their research demonstrate profound injustice—an inequity of such longstanding that the scholars who dared to point it out would be greeted with dismay. Kramer tried to explode the "myth" of women's language as mere stereotype, but one of Lakoff's axioms is that there can be no stereotype without a grain of truth at the core: "for a stereotype to exist, it must be an exaggeration of something that is in fact in existence and able to be recognized. . . ."[36] Political cartoonists work from the same principle: a caricature must contain some semblance of the original for the person to be recognized though the more salient features may be grossly exaggerated.

Lakoff wins the argument about stereotypes on semantic grounds, for by definition a stereotype is a copy of something real. Let us substitute the word "myth" and see if Kramer thereby proves her case against the existence of "women's language." My impression is that she is closer to the truth today than she was in 1974, though I still detect many of Lakoff's nine distinctive features in female speech. My fieldwork is absolutely uncontrolled and is drawn from salespeople, students, physicians, drop-outs, lawyers, waitresses, bankers, faculty and, most instructive of all, passengers on the RTD (the Boulder-Denver bus). In the last category I eavesdrop rather than participate, thereby gathering data in an objective, aloof, one might even say "scientific," manner. Most of these women have stopped gushing, apologizing, and otherwise speaking in an ingratiating manner. Only elderly women of the middle class (to judge by dress codes and body language) can routinely be heard to intone the litany of "italic" conversation in which most of the sentences end in a question mark. Father Time, I conclude, has been at work, and He's moving fast for a change.

Lakoff, therefore, seems dated but not obsolete. Sociopolitically viewed, the content of her book is liberated, but her message is more descriptive than innovative. She does not pioneer change in the form of neologisms. She is particularly intransigent on the subject of new pronouns: she singles out pronouns as less amenable to change than nouns, adjectives, and verbs, and says therefore "we should concentrate our efforts where they will be most fruitful." Moreover, she does not consider generic *he* a problem, at least not for linguists like herself. "But many nonlinguists disagree. I have read and heard dissenting views from too many anguished women to suppose that this use of *he* is really a triviality. The claim is that the use of the neutral *he* with such frequency makes women feel shut out, not a part of what is being described, an inferior species, or a nonexistent one." *Neutral* "he"? Lakoff's approval of the nouns *man* and *mankind* can be found on p. 44 of her book, further proof that she is tolerant of generic constructions. Her position is that "an attempt to change pronominal usage will be futile . . . based purely on pragmatic considerations. . . ."

That sounds sensible, but what follows is both impractical and proprietary:

> I think . . . that linguists should be consulted before any more fanciful plans are made public for reforming the inequities of English. Many of these are founded on misunderstanding and create well-deserved ridicule, but this ridicule is then carried over into other areas which are not ludicrous at all, but suffer guilt by association.[37]

Whereupon she launches into an attack upon *her-story,* or rather upon those who think that using this neologism instead of *history* would help women gain a handle on world affairs. This approach, she claims, is to confuse cause with effect: anteaters are so called because they eat ants, not the other way round. The etymology of *history* (of Greek origin) has nothing to do with the English masculine possessive pronoun *his.* (Quite true.) From *history* she proceeds to attack *himicanes* for *hurricanes.* "If this sort of stuff appears in print and in the popular media as often as it does, it becomes increasingly more difficult to persuade men that women are really rational beings."[38] Note that the protasis of the preceding sentence (the "if " clause) makes no sense, and the apodosis (the main clause) sounds desperate.

Should we really consult linguists before coining new words? Lakoff and I can safely consult ourselves while a lot of the rest of you may demonstrate linguistic naïveté and therefore drag us experts and other innocents into guilt by association. (I'll take the Fifth on that—Amendment, not bourbon.*) The crux is that linguists are seldom consulted about neologisms since there is no national academy in the United States that decides upon the fitness of a word before it can be entered in a dictionary. More to the point, Lakoff is acting here as "arbiter of morality, judge of manners"—a role she declined to assume earlier because it constituted the main function of "ladies."

There is a schizoid aspect to *Language and Woman's Place* in evidence here. In Part I the author defends herself against those who have attacked her view of chivalry as a sham—a poor substitute for real status, power, and authority. In Part II we find a cautionary conclusion—warnings against flamboyant and irresponsible neologisms that feminist nonlinguists coin at their peril because they are used as evidence that women are, as men have always assumed, daffy. At the beginning of the book Lakoff is beleaguered vis-à-vis thoroughly traditional women, who are content with their place on the pedestal; at the end she turns against feminists who would tamper with the language frivolously.

Some pedestal ladies are still around, but they no longer seem to constitute the majority. The consciousness-raising that took place in small groups and was then reported in the press to the extent that everyone could be exposed to its tenets willy-nilly has seriously undermined the naïveté that pervaded women's minds in the fifties and sixties.** Chauvinistic shell games are seen for what they are even by

*I am falling into Lakoffese here, an attempt to appear hip though trained in dead languages. Cf. *LAWP*, p. 52: "almost no one I know of my age and general educational status would be caught dead saying 'divine,' and some even claim not to be able to identify 'magenta,' *while knowing what a universal joint is (in their car, rather than their roach clip)."* (My italics) In point of fact, Lakoff's style is both contemporary and colorful, virtues that helped to promote the content of her book.

**"Willy-nilly" should have been exposed as a sexist construction, but no one seems to have picked on it yet. *The Oxford English Dictionary*, Vol. XII, p. 143, gives the following etymology: "=*will I, nill I* (he, ye) 'be I (he, ye) unwilling'. . . ." Note the absence of

those who do not intend to go to the barricades in the name of equality.

The second issue (tampering with the language) has developed two
strands: (1) crazy neologisms that are linguistic absurdities, invented
for fun and to drive home the message that inequality can be perceived and pointed out (though not necessarily corrected) through
new words; and (2) the continuing serious issue of nonparellel constructions, including *he, man,* and *mankind.* Lakoff accepted the latter
three as innocuous—something that no feminist would now endorse.
Her attitude toward "Ms." as a term of address is also worth noting:
"One must distinguish between acceptance in official use and docu-
ments, where Ms. is already used to some extent, and acceptance in
colloquial conversation, where I have never heard it. I think the latter
will be a long time in coming, and I do not think we can consider Ms.
a real choice until this occurs."[39] This neologism has become part of
the language; one hears (as well as reads) it every day. What did Lakoff mean by "a long time"? "Ms." made its way into English in a relatively short time as measured by historical linguists. Her prediction
here seems too pessimistic; more important, it illustrates her thesis
that language change follows social change, not the reverse. This assumption is made explicit in her discussion of the word *black,* "a term
coined to elicit racial pride and sense of unity," used both in formal
contexts and in the media, "and increasingly in colloquial conversation." This new term, she asserts, does not disprove her argument, for
by the time it was first used (the late sixties "or even 1970") people
were well aware of the civil rights struggles of the early sixties; the acceptability of a new term was already assured by the sympathy toward
the group and its goals. "The parallel to the black struggle should indicate that social change must precede lexical change: women must

"she" here, yet the first definition (where willy-nilly is used as an adverb) states:
"Whether it be with or against the will of the person or persons concerned; whether
one likes it or not; willingly or unwillingly, *nolens volens.*" The second definition (where
it is used as an adjective) makes my point more obvious: "That is such, or that takes
place, whether one will or no . . . ," followed by an example from Tennyson: "And
someone saw thy willy-nilly nun Vying a tress against our golden fern." The second citation (from *Cornhill Magazine,* 1880) is similarly sexist: "All willy-nilly spinsters went to
the canine race to be consoled." The nun is obviously out of her habit or she couldn't
be seducing the fern with her tresses, and, my goodness, spinsters at a dog track! But
that's not the point. The etymology clearly excludes *will she, nill she,* and I assume it's
correct. Purists may wish to avoid this somewhat archaic construction in future.

achieve some measure of greater social independence of men before *Ms.* can gain wider acceptance." She may be right on this point; I cannot remember the first time I heard "Ms." used in conversation. Certainly the acceptance of this title has gone hand in hand with "greater social independence of men." Her final word on "Ms." demonstrates that her definition of its success depends upon the death of "Miss" and "Mrs.":

> Until society changes so that the distinction between married and unmarried women is as unimportant in terms of their social position as that between married and unmarried men, the attempt in all probability cannot succeed. Like the attempt to substitute any euphemism for an uncomfortable word, the attempt to do away with *Miss* and *Mrs.* is doomed to failure if it is not accompanied by a change in society's attitude to what the titles describe.[40]

"Ms." has been accepted; "Miss" and "Mrs." have remained. Lakoff could very well argue that her original contention is correct, that we are currently in a state of transition, and that "Miss" and "Mrs." will disappear in favor of "Ms." only when a woman's status as married or unmarried is considered secondary to her role as a citizen.

The use of titles (including "Ms.") will be taken up in another chapter, as will generic *he.* One may agree or disagree with Lakoff on either of these topics, but it is more interesting to see whether people have accepted her major thesis—that such a thing as "women's language" exists. I believe that they have, else why did so many courses in assertiveness training sprout up in the intervening decade?

When an issue is discussed in the *National Enquirer,* one may safely assume that it has penetrated the public consciousness. See Tom Smith, "How Women Should Talk So Others Take Them Seriously," *National Enquirer,* Oct. 6, 1981, p. 28, which appears to be an interview (or interviews or telephone calls) between the author and two "speech specialists," one of them Robin Lakoff. The other is Dr. Ruth Moulton, "a New York expert who conducted a study on the ability of women to speak in public [and] says that many women are taken advantage of because their speech reveals they're passive—they don't want to be considered disagreeable or 'unladylike.'" All of the advice in the article, whether attributed to Moulton or to Lakoff, can be found in *Language and Woman's Place.*

Assertiveness Training was reported much earlier by the women's magazines. See Marcia Feldman, "Learning To Speak Up," *McCall's*, Oct., 1974, p. 49, which describes a ten-week course called "Assertiveness Training for Women" offered by the Division of Continuing Education of George Washington University. It is not surprising that the course was taught by a man—Dr. Roland Tanck, a psychologist. The participants were torn between excessive politeness and explosions of anger; their statements supply further evidence that women were socialized to be doormats ("ladies") and felt both guilty and fearful whenever they expressed a desire to do something for themselves.

Similarly, Matina Horner's work on "the motive to avoid success" pinpointed female anxiety in test-taking situations when in competition with males, and we now have courses in "Math Anxiety" that are generally aimed at women, since men are not usually thus afflicted.

Lakoff proved her case that "women's language" exists, given the qualifications she made about the nature of her sample and the way she collected her data. She said that not all women spoke this language, but that some men did; that age and socio-economic status made a difference; and that times were changing. Despite criticisms that may and have been leveled at aspects of her impressions of the way some American women spoke in 1975, her book has stood the test of time. *Language and Woman's Place* is still in print, and it is the most cited work in the field. It is virtually impossible to pick up a book dealing with women and language without finding a reference to Lakoff. Whether the author agrees or disagrees with her thesis, Lakoff is mentioned. She is often given credit as the springboard for an author's work. Even when not cited, she is clearly the source for many who have taken up one or another of her ideas for use in an article.* In her intent to be a goad to future research, Lakoff has been wildly successful.

Her success can be attributed to the "resonance" factor: no matter what methodology an author uses (in Lakoff 's case it is random, idiosyncratic, and unauthorized by the canons of social science), if it strikes a harmonious chord with "truth" as perceived by thousands of

*For example: "It used to be that only women qualified their speech. *It's a well-documented fact* that women 'make nice' verbally—by speaking softly, turning statements into questions and adding polite phrases such as 'are you sure' and 'if it's not too much trouble.'" See Jeane Gonick, "Plain, Like Speaking: You, too, can sort of master the babble of, like, indecision," *The Sunday Denver Post, Contemporary*, October 28, 1984, p. 6. (My italics.) The author does not cite Lakoff (or any other linguist) in her article.

readers, there is a note of validity to be pondered. I have been pondering her eighty-three pages for more than ten years now, starting from a position of total agreement with every word she wrote, to gradual skepticism about certain statements, to renewed appreciation of her boldness for stating what she believed in 1975 and hitting upon virtually all the major issues with wit and aplomb. She did not limit herself to "sexist language" or to "women's language" but wove these concepts together into an engrossing essay.

Is "women's language" part of sexist language"? That is a question that she does not address directly. But by implication, she seems to be saying that it is. If "women's language" is now on the way out, "sexist language" has become a growth industry by comparison. It is no longer chic, and it is subtler than it was in 1975, but to assume that language will change as our social condition improves is to accept a view of progress in history that has been halted since 1980 and given official cause for concern since June 30, 1982, with the death of the Equal Rights Amendment.

2

Crossing the Dialect Frontier

If we accept Lakoff 's premise that there is such a thing as "women's language," we must define "language" or run the risk of disqualifying ourself as a professional linguist.* If you speak to someone else, and he or she can't understand you, you are not speaking the same language ("you" here meaning two people.)** This hypothetical situation assumes that neither of the participants has a marked speech impediment or is deliberately speaking double-talk. If you can make out what the other is saying (and vice-versa), but it sounds weird, you two are speaking dialects—that is, variants—of the same language.

Since native speakers of American English can generally make themselves understood regardless of sex, one would conclude that they are speaking the same language. A man may think a woman's speech patterns and her choice of words are strange; in this case a lin-

---

*The use of "ourself" with the "editorial we" that I have used here was routinely employed by E. B. White in *The New Yorker*. Note the lack of agreement within the single word "ourself" so that "we" (plural) can become a "linguist" (singular) at the end of the sentence. I was always amused by this eccentric pronoun "ourself" and have used it here to introduce lack of agreement that to my knowledge never engendered angry protests from readers. Since the prose of *The New Yorker* is considered impeccable and E. B. White an *arbiter elegantarum* as co-author (with William Strunk) of *Elements of Style*, he could get away with this breach of grammatical etiquette, whereas a woman arguing against lack of agreement on the grounds of gender as opposed to number is likely to be chastised. See IV, "Pronoun Envy."

**Note the confusion engendered by the absence of a dual *you* in English. The plural form is used for one, two, or a crowd in the second person. This point is also significant for the discussion of the generic *he* in IV, "Pronoun Envy."

guist might say that they speak different dialects. Dialects exist in both vertical and horizontal forms: vertically in socio-economic class and horizontally in geography. A bank president will most likely speak quite differently from a truck driver in both pronunciation and choice of words. Two bank presidents (or two truck drivers)—one from Maine and one from Mississippi will also differ in the way they express themselves, each one hearing the other as having a somewhat "foreign accent."

The bank presidents and truck drivers are all men (pretend it's 1956). Now we bring in their imaginary wives. Will the trucker's wife talk more like her husband than she will like the banker's wife? (They're all from Mississippi—vertical distinction only.) Yes. Truckers and their wives are more likely to use "ain't," "he don't," and vocabulary items not used by the banker and his wife.

On the other hand, suppose the banker's wife and the trucker's wife meet at a school function and fall into conversation about the kids. They are both housewife-mothers full time, after all. They also share the joy of cooking and the hobby of knitting. They may well begin using tag questions, color terms like *magenta* and *mauve*, euphemisms about the children, and other "womantalk" devices described by Lakoff. Deep into discussion about the relative merits of using foil over a roast turkey (as opposed to a lid or nothing), whether to place the bird upside down or right side up, and exactly what materials should go into a "scrumptious" stuffing, their husbands (if allowed to eavesdrop) might well smile tolerantly and go off to the local bar to pursue "serious" topics like footabll and automobiles ("mantalk"). They don't know and don't really care exactly what their wives are yakking about, though the women demonstrate technical knowledge of their culinary subject.* Men in 1956 might well confess that they didn't understand women, that women were not interested in "important" subjects (politics, for example), and that they indeed spoke a different language.

In this context the word "language" connotes not only syntactic structure, intonational features and technical vocabularies but also an attitude toward the content of what is being said. In short, "Man's World, Woman's Place" (the title of a book by Elizabeth Janeway)

---

*Cooking done by men as a profession, however, was *cuisine*, and the man performing this job in a posh restaurant was a *chef*, not a "mere" cook. His restaurant had a wine steward (never a stewardess), and the serving staff were waiters (never waitresses).

conveys both the vertical and horizontal positions of men and women in the fifties (no sexual overtones intended). People who inhabited different terrains (Maine; Mississippi) or different social realms (bank president's office; the cab of a semi) normally spoke different languages in 1956. Women's locale was the kitchen and the nursery, and the work they did there (however difficult and no matter how great their competence at it) was non-work, i.e., unpaid and without prestige. Women strove for excellence if they wanted to please their husbands and impress other women. Their accomplishments in their "place" were accurately described as "women's work" though it did not count as "real work" at all—a paradox that plunged some thoughtful housewives into depression.

Betty Friedan described this malaise as "the problem that has no name."[1] So far as I know, it never acquired one. Friedan described the symptoms and the etiology without naming the disease. Does "sexism" cover it? "Male chauvinism"? Perhaps. In any case, the reality of woman's "place" was described in negative terms for a change. Friedan blew the cover of "the happy housewife"; no matter how many appliances they had, they were miserable, but having been socialized to feel guilty about their misery, they had kept up a cheerful front—hiding the underlying malaise and exhibiting only secondary symptoms like excessive fatigue, ugly rashes, and moodiness. It is noteworthy that though the problem had no name, it began to be solved when it was aired.[2]

Erma Bombeck fended off neurosis with humor—a genre that requires as much verbal agility as sociological analysis. Whereas Friedan called for a full-scale battle against injustice, Bombeck turned the realities of "woman's place" into a farce, a more acceptable form of social criticism. To hear Bombeck on Friedan in the 80s is instructive for those too young to recall the era of "the happy housewife" or too complacent to appreciate women's position in the early sixties. Bombeck and some of her neighbors drove into Dayton to hear Friedan lecture:

> "She started talking about yellow wax buildup and all that, and all of us started laughing." Friedan shook her finger and scolded them; these were supposed to be demeaning concerns, not funny ones. Bombeck remembers thinking, "God, lady, you can't make it better tonight. What more do you want from us?" Bombeck's feeling was that "first we had to laugh; the crying had to come later." She still has not entirely forgiven

Friedan and other militant feminists. "These women threw a war for themselves and didn't invite any of us. That was very wrong of them."[3]

Perhaps Bombeck also smarts under Friedan's attack against "House-wife Writers," though in 1963 she was not yet syndicated and was therefore not among those named in *The Feminine Mystique.*

> . . . there is something about Housewife Writers that isn't funny—like Uncle Tom, or Amos and Andy. "Laugh," the Housewife Writers tell the real housewife, "if you are feeling desperate, empty, bored, trapped in the bedmaking, chauffeuring and dishwashing details, Isn't it funny? We're all in the same trap." Do real housewives then dissipate in laughter their dreams and their sense of desperation? Do they think their frustrated abilities and their limited lives are a joke?[4]

This condescension toward not only housewife-writers but housewives in general cost Friedan and other confident feminists the ratification of the Equal Rights Amendment, even though they had Erma Bombeck on their side. (According to the article in *Time,* she took off two years to campaign vigorously for its passage.) My theory is that even Bombeck couldn't swing enough of the housewives away from Phyllis Schlafly. The language of the more radical feminists had already turned them off in droves.

Friedan and Bombeck are actually on the same team, and Friedan has revised her earlier attitude towards housewives in *The Second Stage,* where she coined the phrase "the *feminist* mystique."[5] In retrospect she sees the early years of the movement as understandably but wrongly set against the family, for which opinion she was branded by some as a traitor.

The above quotations prove not only that women are behaving like human beings but that they are talking like human beings too. They assert themselves and take the heat, just like a man. Moreover, Bombeck demonstrates not only that housewives can be feminists but that feminists can have a sense of humor. She not only "gets" jokes, she makes them. (Remember that one of Lakoff's nine criteria for "women's language" was that women could neither tell jokes nor understand them.)

Some time between 1963 *(The Feminine Mystique)* and 1984 American women seem to have "crossed the dialect frontier." The phrase comes from *The Demons* by Heimito von Doderer and describes what I think has happened to millions of women in the United States who have been sensitized to the inaccuracy and inadequacy of the language they have traditionally used. To get away from the "woman question" with its political overtones, I have chosen to illustrate language change as change of mentality through a male character in *The Demons*— Leonhard Kakabsa.[6]

Leonhard decides to study Latin, a most unusual step for a blue collar worker in Vienna during the twenties. He comes from a working class family and has had the limited practical education typical of his class, which distinguishes him sharply from other major characters in the book, most of whom are academicians trained at the Institute for Austrian History and bear the title of "Herr Doktor." (Doderer himself was a graduate of this illustrious institute.)

It is noteworthy that Leonhard does not embark upon the study of Latin for either social or political reasons. He is more than content with his job in a webbing factory; he enjoys the company of his fellow workers; and he is proud to be a member of this class. Although he lives in a modest furnished room in a poor section of Vienna (he could afford nothing else, given his wages), he does not buy a Latin grammar to prepare himself for a white collar job. His purchase is almost fortuitous: the bookstores are normally closed before and after his work shift; a change in his schedule means that he can stroll into Fiedler's bookstore for a change. There is also the attraction of Fiedler's buxom daughter, Malva, who works in the store. Old Fiedler himself is a scholarly man. It is he who advises Leonhard on which grammar to buy (Scheindler's) and how to set about studying Latin.

Leonhard spent his spare time memorizing Scheindler, "somewhat in the way he might have learned to handle a complicated machine. . . . "[7] At first his command of Latin is limited to paradigms (declensions of nouns and conjugations of verbs) and how some of these are put together—"the grammatical rules of construction," though he was "slow and clumsy at handling these constructions."[8] He was similarly clumsy in his ability to express new ideas in his own tongue, that is, to converse fluently with those who had a middle-class education. As he relentlessly pursued his study of Scheindler, however, the author's descriptions and explanations of Latin grammar forced Leonhard's brain to absorb this highbrow dialect of German.

One night Leonhard dreamed that he was reading a sentence from Scheindler, and it made no sense to him. He remembered it when he woke up, puzzling over what it could mean: "The optative (form expressing a wish) throws every clause into the subjunctive mood, and the fundamental meaning is thereby lost." It was "gibberish," yet he repeated it, feeling uncomfortable, and then repeated it once more. "And in so doing he discovered that he was beginning to think in an entirely new language. Not Latin. But he was thinking differently in his mother tongue."[9]

He had heard this elevated language in speeches, at factory celebrations, at union meetings. This is the way one should speak, Leonhard thinks; it was like pulling oneself up on parallel bars.

> It was not Latin. But it was not actually his mother tongue, not the language he had learned from his mother's lips. With profound astonishment Leonhard realized that he had for some time been reading to himself in that new language (sometimes moving his lips). It had become his customary inner speech. Now he was even dreaming it. Now he was whispering it to himself after awakening. His inner language already hovered on the threshold of his outer speech.[10]

Doderer says that Leonhard had performed "a decisive act . . . nothing less than crossing the dialect frontier, which in Central Europe, at least, marks the beginning of the true life of the mind."[11]

First he was "thinking differently in his mother tongue." Then he begins thinking in a new dialect of German ("not actually his mother tongue"). While he continues studying Latin—a foreign language— he also continues to expand his knowledge of this other form of German, one that allows him to gain control over his comprehension of events, if not of the events themselves. His first experience of what crossing the dialect frontier has done to his mind involves an internal dialogue about three women in his life. They seemed to form a triangle that grieved him, for it meant a loss of freedom. "Here at the tavern table Leonhard now took the second decisive step in his intellectual history—he had already crossed the dialect frontier and now he made his first creative formation in the language whose realm he had newly entered through the good offices of Scheindler, author of his Latin grammar." The three women in the triangle did not all lie in one plane. One of them was only "adjacent," and he hit upon the phrase "adjacent entanglement" to describe her position with respect to the other two women, "and thereby felt a sense of release. He could go home feeling that he was to some extent in control of the situation. Come what might the meaning had been grasped and formulated."[12]

Leonhard's intellect had been fettered by his dialect. Now he began to create phrases out of words that he would hitherto not have used though he had a passive knowledge of many of them. Eventually he becomes fluent in the new dialect so that he can converse at ease with members of the Institute for Austrian History. It should be added that his reading during this formative period of his intellectual growth was not confined to Scheindler. He also read about classical antiquity, purchased an atlas of ancient history, and spent one precious hour every evening after work in the university library.

Though he was in no way unhappy with his job at the webbing factory, he regretted that he had so little time to pursue his studies. Nor did he drop the old dialect, his mother tongue. He merely acquired another one that opened up a new world to him, a dialect that allowed him to understand ancient history and that also came in handy among new acquaintances. Ultimately he becomes librarian to Prince Alfons Croix, who moves Leonhard into his palace in Vienna and underwrites his education at the unversity so that he will have the credential (a doctor's degree) appropriate to his elevated position.

Is Leonhard Kakabsa's "intellectual history" analogous to that of the women who groped their painful way toward articulating "the problem," while Betty Friedan listened, in April 1959? I think it is. In both cases the mind was flexible, open, and searching clumsily for words to express concepts that were only dimly grasped. In both cases too there was a sense of relief when the concept was verbally aired after initial resistance, hesitation, and then conscious decision to go forward into the unknown.

The striking contrast is in the result of the new enlightenment and the new way of speaking between the Viennese worker and the American housewives. Leonhard's intellectual breakthrough brought him praise and respect. In the penultimate chapter of the book ("The Fire") he emerges as a natural leader for his old comrades. On July 15, 1927, a group of Viennese workers struck, cutting off electricity throughout the city and setting fire to the Palace of Justice. General chaos ensues, with police firing on protesters and vice versa, while underworld characters work the crowds. Leonhard, who had no part in the demonstration, is trapped after he leaves the university. He runs into two of his old friends—similarly trapped—and they immediately charge him with finding them a safe route out. "They were saying again and again in their thickest dialect: 'Lead us outa this, Leo, we can't stan' the sight of it no more. The soot [dregs of society] are out, all the soot from the Prater. You don't see no more workers. You must know how to get through, you know.'"[13]

Leonhard has no idea why he has been chosen as savior of the moment; whether his new status as a man of learning plays a part in his elevation to leadership is not clear. In any case, he and his friends lock arms and make their way through the tumultuous streets. Leonhard pauses to kneel down beside the dead body of a policeman, and his terrified friends raise their hands at the pistols pointed at them by two suspicious patrolmen. The dead policeman was Leonhard's best friend; the patrolmen recognize Leonhard's name, for the dead man had spoken of him often. An inspector asks whether they had witnessed the slaying (they had not) and then asks, "'Are you workers?' . . . turning to all three." "'Yes,' Leonard replied. Any other answer, in regard to himself, did not even occur to him."[14]

Then he led his friends safely out of the section of Vienna that was still under siege. He emerges from this incident a hero. He has earned the respect of his comrades, of the police, of Prince Alfons, and the woman he loves, yet the latter two he would not even have met had he not first crossed the dialect frontier.

The experience of Betty Friedan's unhappy housewives was far different. Women who began to articulate their real feelings—feelings they had suppressed for the sake of their families—were not embraced as heroines. Rather, they were greeted by their nearest and dearest with suspicion and hostility; by professionals, with lectures on hormones and women's "natural" role; and by the general public, with apathy or irritation.

Since that first "rap" session Friedan heard in 1959, women have become progressively liberated in thought and speech. Twenty-five years have elapsed, a quarter of a century of social, political, and linguistic consciousness-raising. Robin Lakoff captured "women's language" before it died out as the dominant speech form of "ladies." Yet it is not really dead; it may have merely swooned or suffered an attack of the vapors, from which it could be revived. If the younger generation (ignorant of history and confident of happy endings) should choose domesticity over citizenship, we might well hear "women's language" again.

Betty Friedan records an appalling wave of anti-intellectualism among college women in *The Feminine Mystique.* The entire post-war generation retreated from the hard-won professional victories of their mothers and grandmothers, concerning themselves instead with training for marriage and motherhood. Intellectual fulfillment was replaced by uterine plenitude. This sinister development became apparent to Friedan in 1959 when she returned to her alma mater (Smith), where she stayed for a week and heard this alarming comment from a soon-to-be-retired psychology professor:

> They're bright enough. They have to be, to get here at all now. But they won't let themselves get interested. They seem to feel it will get in their way when they marry the young executive and raise all those children in the suburbs. I couldn't schedule the final seminar for my senior honor students. Too many kitchen showers interfered. None of them considered the seminar sufficiently important to postpone their kitchen showers.[15]

Friedan assumed that this was an exaggeration until she discovered to her horror that this faculty member's perception was confirmed by the students she interviewed. Moreover, she found the same apathy on other campuses, and concluded:

> The one lesson a girl could hardly avoid learning, if she went to college between 1945 and 1960, was *not* to get interested, seriously interested, in anything besides getting married and having children, if she wanted to be normal, happy, adjusted, feminine, have a successful husband, successful children, and a normal, feminine, adjusted, successful sex life.[16]

In isolation the words "normal," "successful," and "happy" seem innocuous even today unless they are defined as being applicable only within the context of domesticity. The adjectives "feminine" and "adjusted," however, have come under heavy fire, for they invariably set a limitation on woman's full potential and an implicit warning that if the female of the species does not "adjust" to her passive role by staying out of the competitive job market and playing second fiddle to males, she will jeopardize the family, the nation, and the world. Or as Phyllis McGinley wrote, "the world runs better when men and women keep to their own spheres. I do not say women are better off, but society in general is."[17] It is women's "mysterious honor and obligation . . . to keep this planet in orbit."[18] It is certainly a mystery to me that as a woman I am both honored and obligated to keep house instead of working outside of it and that if I defy this convention, I may be responsible for intergalactic collision. McGinley's aphorisms reveal the feminine mystique as both illogical and sacerdotal—illogical because women are urged to "keep to their own sphere" for the good of society, yet more than half of society is composed of women; sacerdotal because McGinley has assumed the role of High Priestess handing down judgments that she seems to have obtained directly from God the Father.

Let us hope that most American women are beyond the model of the Stepford Wife (the happy housewife as robot and vice versa) and the tiresome clichés of the prophets of doom. The Stepford Wives all spoke "women's language"—sweet, childlike, gushing, and foolish. Edith Bunker, by comparison, sounds like Gloria Steinem, for Edith dared to question Archie's judgment and even defied him on occasion. Women today—married, single, widowed, or divorced—appear to be less fearful of speaking out, less tentative when they do. In short, they have crossed the dialect frontier into a new country of the mind, "a habitable languagescape."[19]

Once women in sufficient numbers crossed the dialect frontier and began speaking freely like human beings, they were imitated by others. Freedom is catching. Constraints in language are like a corset: once the stays are loosened, one breathes a sigh of relief. Eventually the reason for the corset is questioned: Is it really necessary to have an eighteen-inch waistline? Vanity gives way to comfort; gradually the corset is modified into a girdle; the girdle into a garter-belt; the garter-belt into pantyhose. . . .And after pantyhose? (Even pantyhose are uncomfortable, especially in hot weather.) The answer is "nothing," and the analogy in language is "anything goes." Swear and use obscenities with abandon. I would predict, however, that most women won't relinquish pantyhose entirely, nor will they all curse and use obscenities. Dress codes as well as speech codes can have a positive effect upon a person's morale.

Once past the dialect frontier of "women's language," we have a new speech form to practice with. Unlike Leonhard Kakabsa, however, we have to invent it as we go along or at least experiment with untried locutions to express what is in our minds but not yet articulated by anyone. Leonhard had his new dialect ready at hand; we have a new dialect too, seized out of the mouths of men and ready for improvement by us. We are conscious of what we are doing with language now, and conscious of what it has been doing to us: putting us in our place. Women are quite literally equal-opportunity speakers, even if they have not acquired parity in the spheres of politics and economics. We are finally exercising our First Amendment rights, and we are paying for those rights.

There is a long tradition of changing one's language to better one's condition. Consider Shaw's *Pygmalion*, first published in 1912 (or "My Fair Lady," the musical based on the play). Professor Higgins took Eliza Doolittle out of the gutter and made her into a lady by changing her speech patterns.[20] Though an unwilling pupil, Eliza worked diligently (bribed with chocolates) and was purged of her cockney accent. She was also dressed and coiffed like a lady, but she failed her first test, when Higgins took her to his mother's and warned her to confine her remarks to the weather and everyone's health. Carried away by enthusiasm, Liza lapsed into her original parlance when recounting the death of her gin-soaked aunt. Her cover was blown, but Higgins would not give up the project since he had a sizeable bet with Colonel Pickering (author of *Spoken Sanskrit*) that he could pass Eliza off as a lady at a forthcoming ball. As we all know, Eliza succeeded; Higgins took the credit; and Shaw proved his point that phoneticians are essential to the national welfare.

> The reformer England needs today is an energetic phonetic enthusiast: that is why I have made such a one the hero of a popular play. . . .if the play makes the public aware that there are such people as phoneticians, and that they are among the most important people in England at present, it will serve its turn.[21]

At the conclusion of *Pygmalion*, Eliza marries Freddy Eynsford Hill and opens a flower shop. At the end of "My Fair Lady" (1958) Eliza fetches Higgins' slippers in dog-like fashion, tantamount to their becoming engaged, a radical departure from the play.

In both versions, the point is made that by changing one's speech, one changes one's personality. Liza goes through a metamorphosis that Higgins had not predicted: he merely wanted to win a bet. He also anticipates that she will be able to work for a living in respectable surroundings rather than hanging about the streets selling flowers for pennies. The flower girl is no fool: she changes not only her language but her character as well. She begins to stand up for herself rather than running to the arrogant professor at his every beck and call. In a perceptive bit of one-up-manship, Liza tells Higgins that it was not the fine clothes and speech lessons that gave her a new sense of how to behave; it was Colonel Pickering's calling her "Miss Doolittle." That was the beginning of self-respect:

> the difference between a lady and a flower girl is not how she behaves, but how she's treated. I shall always be a flower girl to Professor Higgins, because he always treats me as a flower girl, and always will; but I know I can be a lady to you, because you always treat me as a lady, and always will.[22]

This bit of insight catches Higgins off guard. Furthermore, she says that while Pickering may call her Eliza, the professor must address her as Miss Doolittle. She wants an outward sign of respect from him that he isn't willing to give. She threatens to leave, and it is obvious that she means what she says. She can now do without him. It is a terrible revelation, a blow to Higgins' vanity. He responds, amazingly, not with anger but with a speech in behalf of women's liberation:

> "You call me a brute because you couldn't buy a claim on me by fetching my slippers and finding my spectacles. You were a fool: I think a woman fetching a man's slippers is a disgusting sight: did I ever fetch *your* slippers? I think a good deal more of you for throwing them in my face. No use slaving for me and then saying you want to be cared for: who cares for a slave? If you come back, come back for the sake of good fellowship; for you'll get nothing else. You've had a thousand times as much out of me as I have out of you; and if you dare to set up your little dog's tricks of fetching and carrying slippers against my creation of a Duchess Eliza, I'll slam the door in your silly face."[23]

This astonishing bit of rhetoric did not appear in the film; it would have spoiled the "happy ending," with Eliza fetching slippers and the expectation that she will become Mrs. Higgins, "in her place." The movie was made during the era of the feminine mystique. An ending that did not marry off the hero to the heroine was simply not "happy" and had to be changed. But Shaw himself had rejected such a resolution of the plot. He wrote that even though Liza is the heroine of the romance, she has been transformed into a far better creature and therefore doesn't have to marry the hero. Such an ending would have been "unbearable"—drawn from the "ready-mades and reach-me-downs of the ragshop in which Romance keeps its stock of 'happy endings' to misfit all stories."[24]

Changing one's language can be used as a tool for a variety of purposes and is not confined to the crass concept of "upward mobil-

ity" (though I think "downward mobility" is still more crass, particularly if it involves retrogression into the fawning speech of "women's
language" as described by Lakoff and illustrated by Shaw). The hero
in one of Dick Francis's novels deliberately sets out to change his Aus-
tralian accent to an English one and not a "U" English accent but a
lower-class one. His assignment is to uncover a scandal involving the
doping of racehorses; he must pose as a stable boy to obtain inside information. The trouble is that he is from a middle-class family (his father was a barrister), and he himself is the owner of a stud farm. Thus,
he is a gentleman, but a gentleman with a "foreign" accent. To accomplish his purpose he must change his speech both vertically (downward) and horizontally (westward—he flies from Sydney to London
via Asia).

After accepting this assignment from the Earl of October, one of
the Stewards of the National Hunt Committee, Daniel Roke, considers the matter of his accent, though the Earl had told him it wasn't going to be a problem. Here is what Dan ponders after his arrival in
London:

> In the matter of my accent I thought October had been too hopeful,
> because two people, before midday, commented on my being Australian.
> My parents had retained their Englishness until their death, but at nine
> I had found it prudent not to be "different" at school, and had adopted
> the speech of my new country from that age. I could no longer shed it,
> even if I wanted to, but if it was to sound like cockney English, it would
> clearly have to be modified.[25]

He spends the afternoon wandering around asking questions and listening to the answers. "Gradually I came to the conclusion that if I
knocked off the aitches and didn't clip the ends of my words, I might
get by. I practiced all that afternoon, and finally managed to alter a
few vowel sounds as well."[26] By the end of the day no one asks where
he's from, and he himself detects little difference between the barrow
boy whom he talks to and his own "new" accent.

The importance of language was impressed on the hero when at the
age of nine he had moved to Australia and there encountered strange
looks (and perhaps worse) from his new schoolmates. He dropped his
"Englishness" then and there. At the time that the novel opens he is
twenty-seven, yet the hostile reaction to his original accent is still
vivid. Now he must try to recapture it and finds that it's gone. He

must observe, study, and copy what he hears in England, and not from the Earl of October but from working-class men. The significance placed upon the proper vowel sounds among the British is extraordinary to the average American. But fortunately for Dan, he does not have to emulate the "U" accent—which is to some extent standardized—but the "non-U," which is diverse and tainted by regionalism. Therefore, he can approximate a laborer's speech and if it's not quite right, he is thought to be from another part of the island. His wardrobe has been replaced by a stable lad's clothes, and he easily manages to look and act slightly crooked (his intention). His one giveaway is his hands; they're work-worn enough, but when riding a horse he has the "hands of an angel." Otherwise he passes for a stable boy very successfully.

Both Eliza Doolittle and Daniel Roke were aware of the dialects they spoke and consciously changed them for a purpose. In the case of Leonhard Kakabsa, on the other hand, "crossing the dialect frontier" emerged almost as a result of groping for some larger meaning in life before he could have articulated such an objective. He acquired a new dialect of German as a by-product of his Latin study; then he realized that he was now thinking in the new dialect. At length he began to use it and eventually mastered it. In all three cases language alteration had tangible effects in the life of the central character.

I earlier compared Betty Friedan's housewives who discussed "the problem" in April 1959 with Leonhard, for in both cases an unconscious or preconscious entity "dawned" on the mind, and recognition of the entity (that there is a life of the mind) brought relief/release when put into words. If U.S. women have indeed crossed the dialect frontier, then they are aware that "women's language" as described by Lakoff carries with it certain unfavorable connotations whether they have read Lakoff or not. If women want to speak a new dialect, one appropriate to their perceptions about themselves and their society, then they will approach language purposefully as both a sign and a tool of their liberation.

3

*Linguists and Laypeople**

Whereas linguists describe how women talk, laypeople tend to prescribe how women *should* talk. The distinction is an important one: linguistics as a discipline developed as an offshoot of philology, the study of words and phrases in classical texts. For example, a nineteenth-century philologist who published an edition of a medieval author would normally include in his introduction a discussion of the author's "Latinity"—how closely he adhered to the canons of correctness as found in the best classical Romans (primarily Virgil, Cicero, and Caesar). These same canons of "correctness" were imported into English, when grammarians (using Latin authors such as Quintilian) wrote handbooks of our Mother Tongue.

Lexicographers of the English language were similarly preoccupied with presenting only what was "correct," defined as the usage of the upper classes in Great Britain. American dictionaries might have included words that did not appear in the King's English, but they were

*My aversion to "persons" as the plural of "person" is eccentric and antedates the Women's Movement by several decades. I attribute my phobia to an elementary school teacher who made us memorize the Gettysburg Address. Lincoln's phrase "that government of the people, by the people, for the people, shall not perish from the earth" struck me as perfect; I was apparently "imprinted" for life with this locution. A journalist's explanation to me that "persons" sounded more "caring" (as in "Six million persons died in the Holocaust") failed to change my mind. My preference is shared by the National Rifle Association, whose immortal bumper sticker reads: "GUNS DON'T KILL PEOPLE. PEOPLE KILL PEOPLE." In any case, "people" is sex-indefinite and therefore should be viewed tolerantly by linguistic revolutionaries.

nevertheless committed to the principle of correctness, as derived from speech and writing of the educated upper classes.

That class consciousness still exists on this side of the Atlantic (despite our militant opposition to monarchy) is proven by Fran Lebowitz in her mock-serious diatribe against nonsmokers:

> As a practicing member of several oppressed minority groups, I feel that I have on the whole conducted myself with the utmost decorum. . . .I call attention to this exemplary behavior . . . to emphasize the seriousness of the present situation . . . [which] makes it virtually impossible to smoke a cigarette in public without the risk of fine, imprisonment or having to argue with someone not of my class.
>
> Should the last part of that statement disturb the more egalitarian of you, I hasten to add that I use the word "class" in its narrower sense to refer to that group more commonly thought of as "my kind of people."

For more, see "When Smoke Gets in Your Eyes . . . Shut Them," *Social Studies* (New York: Pocket Books, 1982), p. 114.

A great furor arose in the 1960's when Noah Webster's venerable dictionary went into its third modern edition: the Second (published before World War II) was prescriptive and exclusive; the Third was descriptive and inclusive (it listed obscenities).[1]

Webster's notorious third edition reflected the influence of linguists—scholars who wanted to tell it like it was rather than telling it as it should be. Linguists, then, can be seen as rebels committed to informing people what their language is really like instead of perpetuating artificial rules that are frequently based on Latin and often irrelevant to English. For example, the rule about not ending a sentence with a preposition was based upon the etymology of the word "preposition" itself—in Latin, "that which is placed before [its object]". The phrase "the girl I danced with" *should* be "the girl with whom I danced." Most people don't talk that way, but the rule was staunchly retained in grammar books. Winston Churchill once wrote, "A preposition is a good word to end a sentence with," thus showing how much he revered the rule. He also said, "It is me" not "It is I" (another no-no). Churchill attributed his skill in writing English prose (which was considerable) to his flunking Latin early on and therefore having more time to spend on his mother tongue. Aristocrats like Churchill may speak as they please, for they are the models used by lexicographers.

Americans have been slow to give up their traditional Puritanism in matters linguistic. Even now letters from men as well as women can be found in newspapers and magazines deploring a "vulgar" usage or a newly minted word. These self-appointed judges tend also to prescribe how young people should cut their hair and what TV programs are suitable for a family audience. Rock music, drug abuse, and sexual license are routinely attributed to "permissiveness" in language, as if regulation of the Mother Tongue is the Plymouth Rock upon which the ship of state is moored. Or, as Geoffrey Nunberg has so aptly said:

> The linguists are at least forthright in their rejection of linguistic morality. Their opponents, the defenders of traditional values, are more deceptive. They talk a great deal about morality, but in millenarian tones, as if the rules of grammar were matters of revealed truth rather than the tentative conclusions of thoughtful argument.[2]

The fact that language changes, despite the best efforts of English teachers, has only been recognized in this republic since World War II. Consequently, there was still enough of the old purist mystique around to surface when women began to experiment with the language in the name of liberation during the late sixties and early seventies.

The invention of "Ms." is a good example. Its appearance was heralded with the same enthusiasm as the Black Death. There was no place for it on printed forms; therefore, the government and the whole free enterprise system would founder (analogous to the disappearance of paper clips apparently). No one knew how to pronounce it, so it couldn't be used in conversation (that should have killed it off immediately). Alma Graham wrote that there were arguments as to whether it should be "miz," "mis," or "em es."[3] How "mis" would distinguish itself from the pronunciation of "miss" is not clear, though by now irrelevant anyway. Remember that Robin Lakoff reported she had never heard "Ms." pronounced, and that was in 1975. Now we routinely hear and say "miz" without danger of public flogging, nor has the institution of marriage disappeared because this revolutionary word has entered the language. "Ms." is a combination of "Miss" and "Mrs.," and Graham entered the etymology as coming from the word "mistress."[4]

Since both "Miss" and "Mrs." come from "mistress," perhaps it is quibbling to say that the layperson sees it first and foremost as a graphic combination of the two, i.e., as a truly new word. It was not strictly new in pronunciation, however, at least not in the South where it had existed as a variant of "Mrs." for years. Perhaps that is one of the reasons it was accepted: to part of the population it was already familiar. The big advantage of "Ms." in written form, however, was apparent to secretaries all over the United States. When receiving a letter from a woman whose marital status was uncertain, you didn't have to agonize over whether to use "Miss" or "Mrs." in replying: you could fudge by using "Ms." The use of "Ms." did not change anyone's marital status; it merely ignored it.

Nevertheless, "Ms." did have an effect on reality. Whether greeted with enthusiasm or disfavor by women recipients of letters using this title, it forced them to reconsider the alternatives and reflect upon the fact that, like "Mr.," "Ms." concealed marital status. Preservers of the language (i.e., of the status quo) might argue that "Ms." was a vulgar neologism, but they ultimately failed to persuade the general public that it should be avoided. To see how far women had to come even to be presented with this alternative title, one has only to consult Emily Post, where rules of usage are as prescriptive as those in a grammar book:

> On the telephone, a lady says to another whom she knows socially, but who is not on a first-name-calling basis, "Hello, Mrs. Knox? This is Mary Bailey."
> Mrs. Knox answers, "Good morning, Mrs. Bailey!"[5]

This bit of dialogue might still be heard, but compare what Post says about unmarried women:

> Whether she is half-grown or an elderly spinster, calling an unmarried daughter, sister, or aunt *"Miss Mary" is socially correct everywhere,* and not alone characteristic of the South. To ask for "Miss Gray" or even "Miss Mary Gray" would imply either that she is living away from home, or that the person asking for her is a stranger probably calling on business. In any case, it definitely would proclaim a stranger to her family.[6]

It is apparent from this injunction (which sounds like *Gone With the Wind*) that an unmarried woman was perennially addressed as a child, yet from a perusal of married women's property rights in the nineteenth century one learns that when a "Miss" became a "Mrs.," her name, her property, the custody of her children, and her earnings outside the home all belonged to her husband, who, by virtue of his position as male head of household, had the right to use "moderate" chastisement on her if she disobeyed him. In short, married women were treated more like children (more like slaves, really) than were single women. In other words, etiquette books do not necessarily reflect current usage any more than grammar books and dictionaries do.

Or did, at any rate. Alma Graham's riveting article on the making of a nonsexist dictionary shows how a group of creative scholars discovered data in the sources that went far beyond the immediate demands of the project. To quote but one conclusion from this survey of children's textbooks that demonstrates the far-reaching implications of their dictionary, consider the following:

> Obviously, the basic imbalance in male/female pairs was far more than simply a numbers game. The 700,000 computer citation slips contained the evidence that boys and girls were also being taught separate sets of values, different expectations, and divergent goals. Boys in the schoolbooks ran races, rode bicycles, drove fast cars, and took off in spaceships for Mars. Girls, on the other hand, were less concerned with doing than with being.[7]

Graham's conclusions were confirmed by other scholars. See, for example, Marjorie B. U'Ren, "The Image of Women in Textbooks," in which she noted that primary school textbooks were heavily weighted with active male characters, not only physically but intellectually active as well:

> Invariably the father solves problems in the world as well as within the family; he is presented as the builder, the controller, and the creator and executor of ideas. This produces a striking contradiction with reality. Most of our elementary teachers are female, but all of our primary texts bear the message that it is men rather than women who work with ideas and who seek, gain, and dispense knowledge. *Even the illustrated cartoon figures used to indicate and enliven points of grammar are male.*[8]

Mothers, by contrast, are "basically uninteresting." Not only is the mother figure limited to housekeeping and cooking, she is not even allowed significant verbal achievement: " . . . she plays foil to her husband by setting him up for his line. It is mother who asks what can be done and invites a speech from father."[9] This routine was the recommended conversational gambit in *Seventeen* magazine, which I read avidly in the fifties for tips on fashion, makeup, and behavior in mixed company. Never, under any circumstances, should you display your own knowledge; always confine your remarks to questions about your date's expertise. Smile, bat your eyelashes, and murmur, "That's fascinating!" even if you already know the answer to your question. With this training, it is small wonder that when the teenager became a mother, she would continue her "dumb" act.

U'Ren found an interesting double standard outside the textbooks she studied, the *justification* for showing girls in a domestic "helping" context while boys became heroes through acts of derring-do:

> Some have raised the argument that girls face a more domestic and routine adulthood than their male counterparts, and that it is therefore appropriate to present girls with stories about what is likely to be their future experience. Yet stories for boys are not restricted by this same "reality" concern. There are no stories which treat of or anticipate an office job, none which touch on the reality of the factory line or glorify the role of the salesman. Boys, on the contrary, are encouraged to aim for those levels of achievement that our society most values, though in fact most males will have routine adulthoods, devoid of the high adventure they have been taught to dream of.[10]

In one of the few appearances of a woman intellectual—Madame Curie—she seems to be "little more than a helpmate for her husband's projects." The illustration shows her "peering mildly from behind her husband's shoulder while he and another distinguished gentleman loom in the foreground, engaged in a serious dialogue."[11]

Elizabeth Fisher came to similar conclusions—that boys were shown in active roles, girls in passive ones—in children's books in general.[12] And beyond textbooks and children's literature evidence began to be published that showed that the whole process of socializing children, even in societies that were illiterate, appeared to perpetuate this active/passive dichotomy. Nancy Chodorow, in a long article that analyzed studies conducted by sociologists, anthropologists, and psychologists, showed that a girl could be a tomboy while prepubertal but that society frowned upon her if she did not conform at the proper age. "She is supposed to begin to be passive and docile, to become interested in her appearance, to cultivate her abilities to charm men, to mold herself to their wants."[13] Chodorow concludes:

The tragedy of woman's socialization is not that she is left unclear, as is the man, about her basic sexual identity. This identity is ascribed to her, and she does not need to prove to herself or to society that she has earned it or continues to have it. Her problem is that this identity is clearly devalued in the society in which she lives.[14]

This conclusion contains linguistic implications, for if a girl is expected to be "passive and docile," "interested in her appearance," and "charming," she is being prepped for unassertive speech, empty-headed conversation, and silly-seductive question-posing. By learning this language she wins the battle and loses the war.

A whole generation of girls were groomed for the marriage market after World War II by acting like fools. That they succeeded is proven by the Baby Boom. However, it seems strange that there was no awareness of brainwashing, no revolt against second-class citizenship among girls such as could be found among men in the black community. Servitude was apparently beautiful, at least among female white middle-class teenagers; it wasn't called servitude either. Marriage was "natural," "fulfilling," and even patriotic. In the cause of the nation's welfare, women were educated *against* the idea of true education. "The feminine mystique has made higher education for women seem suspect, unnecessary and even dangerous."[15] Thus wrote Betty Friedan in 1963, and she blamed administrators for turning intellectually respectable courses into classes in "life-adjustment." One important target of opportunity was Lynn White, jr. (Professor Emeritus of UCLA but President of Mills College in the fifties), author of *Educating Our Daughters*. White (whom Friedan labeled "the educational protector of femininity") had come to the conclusion that the kind of higher education offered to women was irrelevant to the sort of life they would be leading after graduation. They should not be educated like men; they should be trained for housewifery. The core of women's curriculum should be "the Family" (the hubcap, as it were), from which "spokes" would radiate out to nutrition, textiles, interior decoration, "applied botany," and child-development.[16] Friedan's opinion of this curriculum is both predictable and justified:

> The sex-directed educator is hardly impressed by the argument that a college curriculum should not be contaminated or diluted with subjects like cooking or manual training, which can be taught successfully at the

high-school level. Teach them to the girls in high school, and "with greater intensity and imagination" again in college.[17]

In short, under the rubric of "higher education," middle- and upper-class women were to be groomed for "real life"—wife of a corporate executive and mother of future corporate executives. That there was nothing "higher" about this program than what the girls had already received at the secondary level is glaringly apparent. That "real life" for a bourgeois woman was preordained to exclude a career is also obvious. Young women who considered the life of the mind as "real life" and marriage and motherhood a side issue were sadly out of step with the prevailing wisdom.

Not all of them knuckled under to the demands of domesticity, however. Some went on to graduate or professional school, pursuing what they considered the "truth" while hearing propaganda about "woman's nature" from the citadels of learning as well as the popular press. For young women who came of age after World War II and before the Women's Movement, our Mother Tongue was the "Newspeak" that George Orwell invented for his novel *Nineteen Eighty-Four*. Newspeak is the language of lies, after all, as in "WAR IS PEACE; FREEDOM IS SLAVERY; IGNORANCE IS STRENGTH." The last two seem especially applicable to women in the post-War era. Orwell was aware of the power of words and the danger of totalitarian gibberish from both the Left and the Right. The best protection against "Newspeak" is common sense: if you know what the two words in each sentence mean, you can't possibly make a meaningful equation.

"In prose, the worst thing one can do with words is to surrender to them. When you think of a concrete object, you think wordlessly, and then, if you want to describe the thing you have been visualizing you probably hunt about till you find the exact words that seem to fit." The alternative method promises treachery: "When you think of something abstract you are more inclined to use words from the start, and unless you make a conscious effort to prevent it, the existing dialect will come rushing in and do the job for you, at the expense of blurring or even changing your meaning."

(John Gray, "That Year is Almost Here," *Time,* November 28, 1983, pp. 46–56. Quotation from p. 54.)

Newspeak was already here in 1946, three years before the publication of Orwell's book; we just didn't recognize it. It was a language used on and for women. It made gender more important than species: though recognizing women as human beings, it implicitly branded them as a service class, indispensable for breeding and keeping up the home front for their soldier-husbands in the battlefield-marketplace, but otherwise boring, insignificant, and tolerable only if they could be kept busy and helpful—in other words, a retarded version of the male of the species.

In the fourth century B.C. Aristotle declared that women were deformed males. Aristotle (384–322 B.C.) is frequently cited as the originator of the idea that women are "deformed" males but seldom quoted at length. Here (in translation) is what he actually wrote:

> In human beings, more males are born deformed than females; in other animals, there is no preponderance either way. The reason is that in human beings the male is much hotter in its nature than the female. On that account male embryos tend to move about more than female ones, and owing to their moving about they get broken more, since a young creature can easily be destroyed owing to its weakness. And it is due to this self-same cause that the perfecting of female embryos is inferior to that of male ones: they are not any later in developing than the males, as they are in women, for while still within the mother, the female takes longer to develop than the male does; though *once birth has taken place everything reaches its perfection sooner in females than in males—e.g., puberty, maturity, old age—because females are weaker and colder in their nature; and we should look upon the female state as being as it were a deformity,* one which occurs in the ordinary course of nature. While it is within the mother, then, it develops slowly on account of its coldness, since development is a sort of concoction, concoction is affected by heat, and if a thing is hotter its concoction is easy; when, however, it is free from the mother, *on account of its weakness it quickly approaches its maturity and old age, since inferior things all reach their end more quickly,* and this applies to those which take their shape under the hand of Nature just as much as to the products of the arts and crafts.

From, *Generation of Animals,* trans. A. L. Peck (Cambridge: Harvard University Press, 1953), pp. 459–461. (My italics.) The Greek word that Peck translates as "deformity" is (in transliteration) *anapēría.* Other possible translations are "lameness" and "mutilation." See Henry George Liddell and Robert Scott, *A Greek-English Lexicon,* 9th ed. (Oxford: Clarendon Press, 1940), pp. 1401–1402.

Aristotle is instructive not only for the word *anapēría* but for the whole discussion of male vs. female development. More males are born deformed because male embryos move around in the womb and are therefore subject to fracture (active vs. passive); female embryos take longer to develop (slow vs. fast); once born, however, the female matures more rapidly than the male, but this precocity is interpreted as a *defect*, a *deformity*. It is "on account of its weakness" that the female quickly attains maturity and old age "since inferior things all reach their end more quickly. . . ." One need not be a logician to see the speciousness of this argument. Simply put, females mature more rapidly than males because they are weak and inferior!

Note that there is no explicit reference to the female's "deformity" as consisting in the lack of a penis. It was Freud who made the explicit connection between the female's "natural" inferiority and her being born penis-free.

In the thirteenth century, Thomas Aquinas paraphrased Aristotle, saying that the female was a "misbegotten male" and therefore concluded that although women were necessary for reproduction, in every other area of life (particularly if it required intelligence), a man was one's only suitable assistant. Freud described women as deformed males too, making "penis envy" a household word and a well-developed superego the exclusive possession of men. None of these three luminaries located the brain in the penis, but they might as well have.

It is ironical that there exists a certain prejudice against "dumb jocks" as if physique prevented intellectual development in the case of athletic men. Logically, then, women's smaller musculature should have fostered the idea that whatever they lacked in brawn could well develop in the form of brain. But no. Women were physically *and* intellectually inferior. Act weak, helpless, and dumb (said the teen magazines of the fifties), and you'll attract a handsome boyfriend. Above all, do not reveal your intelligence. Keep your mouth shut except to ask questions that will make your man look brilliant. He gets the credit for brains, but you get the envy of the other girls. Not penis envy, but envy of the perks that automatically come with a penis: status, prestige, power, authority, and a career.

Note that Aristotle was a pagan, Aquinas a Roman Catholic, and Freud a Jew. They seem to have little in common except their assessment of women as defective men. It is certainly true that women lack a penis, but it could also be said that men lack a womb and are therefore defective women. If Aristotle, Aquinas, and Freud had been born female, they would undoubtedly have taken just this position: defining the opposite sex to the advantage of their own.* Let us accept the fact that these famous philosophers, three of the principal thinkers in the history of Western Civilization, agreed that women were inferior to men.

Women began to rebel against this caricature by speaking out. No one knows when the first woman opposed a male's statement with a flat, "That isn't true," or what happened to her when she did. The trouble with women is that they have not conformed to the dogmas of Aristotle, Aquinas, and Freud. Total acquiescence becomes tiresome after a while. In the late sixties and early seventies, women who had read Friedan and other subversive writers started expressing their dissatisfaction with our Mother Tongue. Linguists and laypeople got into the act, pointing out "sexism" in language (a new word at the time) and making suggestions for change.

Activists brought their findings to the attention of publishers— especially publishers of children's textbooks—and guidelines for purging sexism were generated for authors who wanted to update their prose.[18] Scott Foresman was the first to enter the fray with "Guidelines for Improving the Image of Women in Textbooks" (1972), followed by McGraw-Hill, whose "Guidelines for Equal Treatment of the Sexes . . . " (1974) covered both textbooks "and nonfiction works in general."[19] The assault against sexism had already been pioneered by the verbal war on racism, which is made quite clear from McGraw-Hill's opening sentence:

> The word *sexism* was coined, by analogy to *racism*, to denote discrimination based on gender. In its original sense, *sexism* referred to prejudice against the female sex. In a broader sense, the term now indicates any arbitrary stereotyping of males and females on the basis of their gender.[20]

McGraw-Hill wished to "eliminate sexist assumptions . . . to make . . . staff members and . . . authors aware of the ways in which males and females have been stereotyped in publications; *to show the role language*

---

*Gloria Steinhem has written a hilarious parody of this sort of reversal—"If Men Could Menstruate." "Sanitary supplies would be federally funded and free. Of course, some men will still pay for the prestige of such commercial brands as Paul Newman Tampons, Muhammad Ali's Rope-a-Dope Pads, John Wayne Maxi Pads, and Joe Namath Jock Shields—'For Those Light Bachelor Days.'" See *Outrageous Acts and Everyday Rebellions* (New York: Holt, Rinehart and Winston, 1983), pp. 337–340.

has played in reinforcing inequality. . . ."[21] Their suggestions are far-reaching and propose to debunk the "masculine mystique" as well as to upgrade the image of women.[22] Some of their specifications seem downright quaint by now, for example: "Instructional materials should never imply that all women have a 'mother instinct' or that the emotional life of a family suffers because a woman works."[23] But much of the material in the "Guidelines" has yet to be realized, despite the fact that they contain reasonable conclusions backed up by facts. "According to Labor Department statistics for 1972, over forty-two percent of all mothers with children under eighteen worked outside the home, and about a third of these working mothers had children under six. *Publications ought to reflect this reality.*"[24]

Commentators were quick to react to this manifesto, though they do not appear to have objected to earlier guidelines banning racism. George F. Will wrote a stinging attack against McGraw-Hill, to the effect that this great publishing house was no longer playing with a full deck.[25] He found the Guidelines a "depressing document" and asserted that "certain intelligent women must cringe at the kind of attention lavished on women" in it. McGraw-Hill "huffs and puffs through 11 pages of proscriptions"—some "embarrassing," some "banal," and others "pathetic."

I did not cringe when I first read the Guidelines, so that makes me an unintelligent woman by definition, nor did I find them depressing —quite the contrary. The "huffing and puffing" of the publisher did not come through to me, nor did Will's labeling of certain locutions as "embarrassing," "banal," or "pathetic." All of the above, however, can be applied to Will's column. He is self-righteous and unconvincing. When he accuses McGraw-Hill's Guidelines of demonstrating "more truculence than evidence," he is simply wrong. His anger shows; he has enlisted in the War of the Words; and his prose is thoroughly martial:

> The McGraw-Hill guideline writers say they just want to "reflect" reality. In fact, they want to change reality, and they think they can do this by tinkering with the language. They are going to pound flat the battlements of injustice, and their hammer will be . . . a sanitized English language.[26]

God forbid that a publisher should urge its authors to "tinker" with the language! And its weapon against sexism is "a sanitized English language." Is this a surreptitious snipe at Kotex or a reference to the "Cordon Sanitaire" of World War I? Perhaps both. Will continues his diatribe with a profound linguistic pronouncement that reveals his sincerity as well as his naïveté:

> Obviously the web of language shapes as well as reflects reality. But McGraw-Hill's guideline writers insist . . . that the sort of commonplace words they complain about have played a significant role in reinforcing the unequal status of women, and that changing the offending words will change the world in significant ways.[27]

McGraw-Hill wins game, set, and match here. The Decade of Our Discontent since Will wrote this column has proven that just those "commonplace" words that he scorns as not worth tinkering with are the very ones that have kept women in their place. And some not-so-commonplace ones, like "aviatrix": "I, for one, do not mind if my airline pilot is female, but I don't want to be taken 38,000 feet up by a pilot who feels insecure in the presence of the word 'aviatrix.' "[28] Well, *I* mind. In 1974 it was a purely hypothetical situation. In the mid-eighties it is not. I quote from the Boulder *Daily Camera*, July 11, 1984, p. 2A: "FIRST WOMAN 747 PILOT" (caption under photo) "Captain Tangela Tricoli, an American Airlines pilot, sits in the cockpit of a Boeing 747 at the Dallas-Fort Worth Airport in Grapevine, Texas. American says Tricoli is the first woman to obtain a 747 rating." There is no mention of her actually *flying* the plane, you'll note, and the location of the airport makes one suspicious. As a nervous passenger under the best of circumstances, I would be very upset if Captain Tricoli smiled at me when I called her an "aviatrix." I would assume that she didn't know the word had gone out with Amelia Earhart and that she might not know that prop jobs had been replaced by jets.

Will continues his lecture on a coy note: "Although I am of the male persuasion, even I understand that the unequal status of women is an irrational waste of talent in most societies." (Including ours? He doesn't say.) He then accuses McGraw-Hill guideline writers of "Stakhanovite witlessness"! This should be crystal clear to everyone; if not, look up Alexei Stakhanov, Russian miner (1905–1977). Then proceed to the following:

> Such niggling about words trivializes that which is not trivial—the cause of female equality. In fact, the niggling done by McGraw-Hill

guideline writers suggests they do not understand that there are some ways of clamoring for "respect" that make it hard for mature people to respect the clamorers. Anyone who feels victimized by role words is inevitably going to be treated, with reason, as a problem child who has no serious worries—or ideas.[29]

Foiled again. Back to the play pen.

Will concludes with a plaintive question (cf. Freud's, "What do women want?"): "What will be left of the language when it has been sanitized so thoroughly that no irrational minority can blame its afflictions on innocuous phrases?" (Read it again; it parses, but not easily.) This question needs no answer. We can all see how concerned the author is to help us poor gals to stop making fools of ourselves. However, Will's landmark decision of 1974 did not deter either scholars or the general public from pursuing or at least enduring the war on sexism. Women are so used to being ridiculed that even George F. Will couldn't persuade them to lay down their arms and go along quietly.

I am persuaded that Will is "of the male persuasion" (as he says in his column); I am further persuaded that anyone who uses the expression "of the male persuasion" is not a respectable model for writers, male or female.

It's easy to write something so irreverent today, yet in 1974 Will seemed to represent the majority. Many women felt threatened by the fact that textbook publishers proposed to change their housewife image. The best article in my files that expresses this fear explicitly is "Militant Housewife Says Baloney to 'Lib'" by Jane Cracraft.[30] There is a large photo of the housewife captioned "MRS. HILMA SKINNER SAYS HOUSEWIVES ARE DISTURBED."* Mrs. Skinner was working to promote HOW ("Happiness of Womanhood"—"an anti-women's lib group in Colorado") in order to fight "the efforts of the National Organization for Women (NOW) to change 'sex stereotyping' in textbooks. NOW wants women portrayed as the doer, not only the watcher; as the athlete, not only the cheerleader; as the doctor, not only the nurse." One wonders why such changes would not be welcomed by all women, but that is to miss Skinner's point. By shifting

*Jane Cracraft did *not* write the caption. Reporters seldom do. Cracraft was with *The Denver Post* (Boulder Bureau) until 1983, when she opened her own business as a legal investigator. She is currently writing a handbook on how to do research in public records. She recommends her new field as an excellent one for women. (Telephone conversation, July 12, 1984)

the focus from hearth and home to the marketplace, housewives were implicitly downgraded:

> We don't want girls to grow up with the idea that there's something wrong with staying home and doing those things [cleaning and baking]. . . . We feel like the working mother can't do justice to either the job or being a mother. We're not against those who want to make a career instead of having a family, or those who are forced to get out of the home because they are the sole support of their children. But whenever possible, the family should come first.

According to Skinner, "HOW is a political outgrowth of 'Fascinating Womanhood,' a philosophy of femininity which encourages women to learn how to please a man." It is also the title of a book by Helen B. Andelin, who promises in her introduction:

> This book will teach THE ART OF WINNING A MAN'S COMPLETE LOVE AND ADORATION. It isn't necessary for the man to know or do anything about the matter. In fact, it is an advantage if he does not. The art is to arouse his feelings. This is not a difficult accomplishment for woman, because it is based upon her natural instincts. In our complicated, highly civilized life of today, many of her natural instincts have become dulled or suppressed. She needs but to re-discover that which belongs to her by nature.[31]

So much for the philosophical basis of HOW; its "main political activity . . . is opposition to the Equal Rights Amendment. . . ." Skinner says she was for it when she first heard about it—"equal pay for equal work and all of that," but she changed her mind:

> . . . I think there's more to it. I'll tell you where it's leading us. It's leading us toward a nation *where women give up their right to have their husband support them, where women become criminally liable for half of the family's income.* (My italics)

When Cracraft asked what part of the Equal Rights Amendment made women responsible for half of the family income, Skinner said, "it isn't in there yet, 'but it's coming.' "

She had a point. The wording of the ERA has not been altered substantially since 1923 when Alice Paul wrote it, nor since its demise in 1982, nor in attempts to resurrect it. The Amendment explicitly states that sex should not be used as a criterion to deprive a person of his or her rights.* It would supposedly make it easier for women to get into traditionally male jobs (i.e., better paying jobs) and therefore tempt housewives away from the hearth. (Women have typically earned sixty cents on the dollar compared to men, and that figure, to my knowledge, has not changed for the better since 1974.) Skinner's two-pronged attack—against the changing stereotypes of women in text-books and against the passage of the Equal Rights Amendment—makes sense.

Cracraft sums up Skinner's opinion in one sentence: "Mrs. Skinner said she thinks the Christian character of America and the strength of the American family is being undermined by social change." Notice how these ideas parallel those of Phyllis Schafly, who had not yet be-come a household word. Some feminists were sneering at housewives in 1974; they were also blaming Christianity as an oppressive patriar-chal religion and fingering the family as women's main obstacle to progress. The pernicious effects of organized religion were pointed out by Mary Daly in *Beyond God the Father* (1973). The family was a still more controversial subject:

> . . . liberated women have shown strength in certain areas where the old feminism was weakest. Laws, customs, and prejudices keep women down, yet even when they don't women still find equality hard to get. There are many reasons for this, but chief among them are the sexual relationships and roles that make women responsible for domestic life. . . .some femi-nists have always known this. Elizabeth Cady Stanton and her associates raised the marriage question, but with such results that leading feminists never again dared confront the issue openly.[32]

Feminist claims may have been on target, but their posture and lan-guage were wrong. Instead of wooing housewives and mothers, they insulted them. This faux pas has been admitted by activists in both parties. On June 30, 1982 the rhetoric of Women's Liberation had to change, or feminism, not just a Constitutional Amendment, might be deader than a doornail.

---

*The entire text of the Equal Rights Amendment is as follows:

Section 1: Equality of rights under the law shall not be denied or abridged by the United States or by any state on account of sex.

Section 2: The Congress shall have the power to enforce, by appropriate legislation, the provisions of this article.

Section 3: This amendment shall take effect two years after the date of ratification.

4

Pronoun Envy

"Pronoun Envy" was the title of an article that appeared in *Newsweek,* December 6, 1971, but it was coined by a linguist, Professor Calvert Watkins, eminent Indo-Europeanist and at that time Chairman of the Department of Linguistics at Harvard. He and sixteen of his colleagues in the department had written a letter to *The Harvard Crimson,* which was published November 16, 1971, and said, in part:

> For people and pronouns in English *the masculine is the unmarked and hence is used as a neutral or unspecified term.* . . . The fact that the masculine is the unmarked gender in English . . . is simply a feature of grammar. It is unlikely to be an impediment to any change in the patterns of the sexual division of labor toward which our society may wish to evolve. There is really no cause for anxiety or pronoun-envy on the part of those seeking such changes. (p. 17; my italics)

This letter from the "authorities" was prompted by an article that had appeared in *The Harvard Crimson* on November 11 entitled "Two Women Liberate Church Course." The two women—Harvard Divinity School students—had called for an end to sexist language in a course they were enrolled in. The teacher, Professor Harvey G. Cox, polled the class about this request, which specifically called for a halt to the use of the nouns *man* and *men* as well as the masculine pronouns to refer to all people. The proposal also asked that masculine names and pronouns be avoided when referring to God. The class voted for these linguistic reforms, which would have remained an intramural matter were it not for the fact that the articles in *The Harvard Crimson*

50

were picked up by *Newsweek.* This lively bit of history can be found in Chapter Five, "The Language of Religion," in *Words and Women* by Casey Miller and Kate Swift.[1]

Miller and Swift did not take Watkins to task for his calling the masculine pronoun "unmarked . . . and hence . . . a neutral or unspecified term." I would have challenged him on this assertion and on another part of his letter that said, "This reflects the ancient pattern of the Indo-European languages. . . ." Since my Ph.D. is in Indo-European linguistics, I was particularly struck by this statement, for an ancient Indo-European pattern seldom has a bearing on English usage today. It is enlightening to learn about the history of a given locution, but it does not follow that whatever has been established as the norm since prehistoric times should be maintained without "anxiety." In other words, descriptive linguistics has been turned into prescriptive linguistics. Mary Ritchie Key, an anthropological linguist, represents a more liberated point of view. After amassing data from various cultures on how language reflects society, she concludes:

> Serious and responsible people can experiment in areas that will encourage rational changes based on patterns of human behavior. Such a process may bring stability to the seeming chaos. Research in languages and linguistic studies allied with male/female social behavior should be undertaken in depth. There is much to be done yet in understanding the universalities of gender systems in all languages of the world. *We don't even understand the gender system in English yet.*[2]

Yet despite our lack of data and our failure to understand the cultural origins of various linguistic phenomena, she does not hesitate to recommend alternatives to sexist expressions.

Miller and Swift argued more persuasively and succinctly than I would have done: they merely quoted Watkins to Watkins and caught him out in an internal inconsistency:

> Professor Watkins was apparently ignoring his own insights on the interaction of language and culture already quoted in Chapter 4.[3]

Chapter 4 includes the following statement by Watkins: "The lexicon of a language remains the single most effective way of approaching and understanding the culture of its speakers."[4] And "[language] is at once the expression of culture and a part of it."[5]

Miller and Swift also quote the shrewd insight of James C. Armo-

gost of the Department of Linguistics at the University of Washington:

> A reasonably inquisitive person might wonder why the masculine is
> unmarked. The question deserves a better answer than: "What a coinci-
> dence that the masculine is unmarked in the language of a people con-
> vinced that men are superior to women."[6]

Ann Bodine, a sociologist at Rutgers, wrote in 1975 that some
grammarians lamented the lack of a sex-indefinite third person singular pronoun in English; others declared that *he* must serve this function; still others said that the masculine *is* the sex-indefinite pronoun.[7]
This last position seems to have been the one adopted by Calvert Watkins when he called the masculine pronoun "unmarked," and therefore "neutral" and "unspecified." Bodine wrote that feminists
objected to the use of *he* when it might be referring to women and
that they thought a substitute ought to be found. "The reaction to
this demand has ranged from agreement, to disagreement, to ridicule, to horror, but invariably the feminists' demand is viewed as an
attempt to alter the English language."[8] Bodine maintained that the
opposite was true: it is the prescriptive grammarians who have been
trying to alter the language for 250 years. The third person plural has
been widely used for a long time because it is sex-indefinite, unlike the
third person singular, e.g.: "(1) Anyone can do it if *they* try hard
enough." "(2) Who dropped *their* ticket?" and "(3) Either Mary or John
should bring a schedule with *them.*"[9] Prescriptive grammarians and
the entire publishing industry (wrote Bodine) have attempted to
"eradicate" such locutions on the grounds of lack of agreement. Note
that in each of the three examples the subject of the main clause is singular *and* sex-indefinite. The pronouns *they, their,* and *them* (being plural) do not agree in number with their antecedents *(anyone, who,* and
either Mary or John). *They, their,* and *them* are sex-indefinite like *anyone,
who,* and *someone,* yet grammarians insisted that the pronoun must
agree in number with its antecedent. Therefore, the only "correct"
form to use was *he, his,* or *him.*

Why? wondered Bodine. She did not think it was a coincidence that
gender agreement was ignored. "Surprising as it may seem in the light
of the attention later devoted to the issue, prior to the nineteenth century 'they' was widely used in written, therefore presumably also in
spoken, English."[10] Usage, however, has not been the yardstick for

prescriptive grammarians since the eighteenth century up to the present, even if some of the users were illustrious writers. "A non-sexist 'correction' would have been to advocate 'he or she' but rather than encourage this usage the grammarians actually tried to eradicate it also, claiming 'he or she' is 'clumsy,' 'pedantic,' or 'unnecessary.' "[11] Neither sex-indefinite *they* nor *he or she* was allowed: only *he* was "correct." For a current definition of "correctness" in American English, see the interesting debate between Dwight Bolinger and William F. Buckley, Jr., "Usage and Acceptability in Language," *The American Heritage Dictionary,* Second College Edition (Boston: Houghton Mifflin, 1982), pp. 30–33. Buckley writes: "mere usage, however prolonged, does not baptize. Providence in due course sometimes accepts into its bosom sinners, but usually only after time served in the antechambers. And how will we know just when that dispensation is granted? Well, to answer that only in part in jest: by asking me" (p. 32). Pope William decides. But I caught His Holiness in an error once on "Firing Line": men (or horses, I can't remember which) were "gam.-bŏl.ing" around. The correct pronunciation is "gám.bəl.ing"; perhaps Pope William thought hoi polloi would confuse it with "gambling" and therefore supplied a spelling pronunciation (a habit of the semi-learned). For a less pontifical opinion, see Dwight Bolinger, ibid., pp. 30–32.

Bodine summarized her findings thus:

> Although the grammarians felt they were motivated by an interest in logic, accuracy, and elegance, the above analysis reveals that there is no rational, objective, basis for their choice, and therefore the explanation must lie elsewhere. It would appear that their choice was dictated by an androcentric worldview; linguistically, human beings were to be considered male unless proven otherwise.[12]

She proved her case with ease and demonstrated that linguistic chauvinism (my phrase) was rampant in 1975. Of thirty-three grammar books being used in American junior and senior high schools, twenty-eight "condemn both 'he or she' and singular 'they', the former because it is clumsy and the latter because it is inaccurate."[13] One of the grammar books she consulted made this astonishing explanation as to why the "awkwardness" of *he or she* should be shunned: "'grammatically, men are more important than women.' "[14] However, if you follow this prescription to its logical conclusion, you may fall into ludicrous hypercorrection. The following sentence was written by a twelve-year-old boy after a "dunking" by classmates: "'When I came up, everybody was laughing at me, but I was glad to see him just the same.' "[15]

Of course, this and similar sentences can be corrected by supplying a plural subject, such as "all the children," for *everyone,* but Bodine has made her point. The use of singular *they* is widespread, but since we have been brainwashed into not using it because of lack of agreement in number, we shrug and assume that usage must be wrong. Even feminist linguists have thought that the pronoun system was too entrenched to be changed—the opinion of Robin Lakoff and also of Nancy Faires Conklin, author of "Perspectives on the Dialects of Women."[16]

Bodine thought that the pronoun had changed in favor of singular *they* more than most people (including linguists) realize. Her proof is in the second person: we now use *you* for both singular and plural. Earlier English had singular *thou-thee* (nominative and accusative) and plural *ye-you* (nominative and accusative). Eventually the accusative plural *you* supplanted the other forms of the second person, proving that pronouns can change after all.

Bodine believed that English developed its second person singular form in the feudal age to be used by persons of superior rank. When the need for a familiar vs. formal second person died out with the feudal system, the plural *you* swept in. She took this explanation from Otto Jespersen's *Growth and Structure of the English Language* (1938; reprinted 1968), but it is not historically convincing. Old English had a well-developed pronoun system in place before the rise of feudalism. The second person alone had twelve forms:

	Singular	*Dual*	*Plural*
Nom.	ðū	git	gē
Gen.	ðīn	incer	ēower (īower)
Dat.	ðē	inc	ēow (īow)
Acc.	ðec, ðē	incit, inc	ēowic, ēow (īow)[17]

That most of these forms dropped out of use (notably the entire dual) indicates a drive toward simplification that is paralleled by the loss of the oblique cases in nouns and adjectives.* Nouns and adjectives also

---

*The oblique cases include all but the nominative. In addition to the nominative, genitive, dative, and accusative cases, nouns and adjectives had a fifth case—the instrumental.

lost their gender (English used to have masculine, feminine, and neuter, like ancient Latin and modern German). I cannot see the simplification of the second person pronouns as a consequence of the rise and decline of the feudal system since other kinds of simplification (including verb conjugations) were also under way that have no particular connection with hierarchical social structure.

Nevertheless, Bodine is convincing in her argument that if the second person pronoun made such a significant alteration, so could the third, if prescriptive grammarians would let it alone. She does not insist that we should switch over to "everyone . . . their" in the name of Women's Liberation. What she does is to suggest that we observe this construction closely over the next few years, since the locution in question has been in our speech and writing for more than 250 years. Even Buckley should think that is enough time in the antechambers waiting for an audience, if not a dispensation.

If Ann Bodine's cautious optimism is prophetic and *vox populi* becomes *vox dei*, singular *they* could replace generic *he* in sentences beginning with *someone, anyone, somebody, anybody, any student, the person who*, etc. At the moment, singular *they* is not so sanctioned. Advice from McGraw-Hill includes the following:

> The English language lacks a generic singular pronoun signifying *he* or *she*, and therefore it has been customary and grammatically sanctioned to use masculine pronouns in expressions such as "one . . . *he*," "anyone . . . *he*," and "each child opens *his* book." Nevertheless, avoid when possible the pronouns *he, him,* and *his* in reference to the hypothetical person or humanity in general.[18]

Suggestions for avoiding these traps include excision of *his* where it is not necessary, recasting the subject as a plural, and replacing the masculine pronoun with "*one, you,* or *he* or *she, her* or *his,* as appropriate. (Use *he* or *she* and its variations sparingly to avoid clumsy prose.)"[19] Singular *they* is missing.

Bodine rightly said that not only the grammarians but also the publishing industry had condemned *he or she* as "awkward." McGraw-Hill gives additional interesting advice:

> To avoid severe problems of repetition or inept wording, it may sometimes be best to use the generic *he* freely, but to add, in the preface and as often as necessary in the text, *emphatic statements to the effect that the masculine pronouns are being used for succinctness and are intended to refer to both females and males.*[20]

George F. Will, who found the whole document "depressing," is correct only about this particular section, which he didn't cite. For a set of guidelines aimed at "equal treatment of the sexes," this lapse into *he* as the final solution strikes me as backsliding. It reminds me of the textbook I had for modern European history as an undergraduate, R. R. Palmer's *A History of the Modern World* (New York: Alfred A. Knopf, 1950). There wasn't much about women in it, only a few female monarchs. A new edition (the fifth) appeared in 1978 with Joel Colton as co-author. I glanced at the index to see if there was now an entry for *women*. There was! I turned to the main pages cited (915–916). (There were eight other entries under *women*, but this was the longest—the "in-depth" survey, as it were.) In one and one-half pages the first and second women's movements were mentioned, with references to the Third World as well. These few paragraphs stressed the importance of women more than once, but the fact that women were allotted so little space in a textbook of 1100 pages tells more about the significance of women than the authors' glowing sentences would lead the reader to believe.

Similarly, when McGraw-Hill says that recourse to generic *he* is sometimes necessary so long as the author stresses in the preface and throughout that *he* is only being used for succinctness and that *he* means both *he and she*, the publisher is acknowledging a debt to history and tradition. I do not accuse them of "bad faith" or assume that McGraw-Hill is/are a fink.* For most people trained to write in a certain way (including me), breaking with tradition can be both painful and awkward. Take the case of *like*. I was taught that under no circumstances was it to be used as a conjunction. The phrase "like I say" was ruthlessly purged from our prose in those dismal six weeks before the New York State Regents Exams. Then Winston cigarettes came out with a new slogan: "Winstons taste good like a cigarette should!" I couldn't believe my eyes and ears. I don't remember the year, but I suspect it was in the early fifties, yet to this day I cannot hear the phrase "like I say" without wincing, nor can I bring myself to use it.

*It is worth noting that the option "McGraw-Hill is" and "McGraw-Hill are" is not only acceptable but *de rigueur* in the British Isles. "The government prefers to postpone its decision" and "The government prefer to postpone their decision" can both be found because the first statement emphasizes government as a collectivity whereas the second stresses it as a group of individuals. That government and other collective nouns may be singular or plural at will though the word is grammatically singular shows that usage among the most literate can defy the convention of numerical agreement.

"As I say" is what I was taught, and "like I say" affects me about the same way that "ain't" does. It sounds uncouth; it grates on my eardrums. In short, I think there is an esthetic factor to be discussed before we accept "anyone . . . their." It doesn't make me wince when I see it or hear it, and I believe Bodine was right when she asserted that singular *they* was far more widespread than we might have suspected, widespread among outstanding writers as well as among the public at large. I predict that it will eventually enter the canons of sanctioned locutions, whereas *he or she* (which is perfectly correct in both number and gender) will not, at least not in writing. If you begin a paragraph with *someone* or *anyone* and continue on for several sentences, each one requiring either *he or she, his or her, him or her,* the paragraph does sound clumsy. Singular *they* (patiently waiting in the antechambers) appears tempting by contrast.

On the other hand, to take McGraw-Hill's advice and "to boldly go" where every man has gone before is fraught with peril. I could not forego the opportunity to quote a well-known split infinitive. If you haven't heard it on "Star Trek," you are probably an alien. Prescriptive grammarians have cautioned against the split infinitive with as much zeal as they have labored in behalf of generic *he.* The reason seems to lie in the fact that you do not split infinitives in Latin and therefore you shouldn't do so in English. The Latin infinitive consists of a single word (e.g., *vincere,* "to conquer") and therefore is incapable of being split. This proves that all older grammarians are not necessarily sexists, since the infinitive contains no hint of gender. (Actually when used as a substantive, the Latin infinitive is considered to be neuter in gender.) That the unfounded taboo against splitting infinitives is still alive is illustrated by columnist Jill Scott, who reported on a letter she had received from a "gentleman lawyer who calls himself an 'amateur grammatical purist'": "This letter was painstakingly done and rather charming, even if his criticisms were out to lunch. He included reminiscences of his own high school English teacher—who ' . . . would have condoned adultery in the school hallways before he would suffer the anguish of a split infinitive!'" Jill Scott's column is called "Essays on Education," and this particular item appeared under the title "Fan Mail: Welcome to the Grammar Lonely Hearts Club," *The Sunday Denver Post, Contemporary,* July 22, 1984, p.46.

We should heed the warnings of psychologists, philosophers, and educators before slouching reverently back toward HE.[21] We should consider the effect of so-called "generic *he*" upon children as well as upon adults. Do school girls perceive any females in *he?* No. Do women feel left out when books contain only the masculine (but supposedly "neutral") pronoun? Definitely.

Psychologist Wendy Martyna has published results of experimental tests that should convince the most hardened linguistic chauvinist.[22] In a paper before the American Psychological Association she explained that of seventy-two students she tested (thirty-six males, thirty-six females) nearly 20 percent did not infer *she* from *he* in comprehending the generic masculine. (She used both statements and accompanying pictures for part of the test.)

> When given a sentence such as "When someone listens to the record player, he will often sing along," and presented with the female version of the appropriate picture, these students responded that the picture did not apply to the sentence. There were no sex differences: eight females and six males returned this judgment.[23]

The explanation of the experimental set-up and its results are somewhat complex to one not trained in social science research (generic me), but I found 20 percent to be a significantly large number of students choosing "not apply" to a generic *he* sentence accompanied by a female picture. All of the grammatical comfort about the "neutral," "unspecified," and "unmarked" character of the masculine pronoun proffered by Calvert Watkins and other members of the Harvard Linguistics Department skirts an important issue: the actual perception of hearers and readers.

Martyna continues:

> The ambiguity of generic "he" is doubly evident. Not only do some students comprehend it as specifically male, and other students as a human referent; but the same students render contradictory judgments, deciding in one instance that "he" includes "she," and in another, that it does not.[24]

She supplies some of the explanations the students gave, first those who chose "not apply" for generic *he* sentences accompanied by a female picture. "Recall," she says, "that *all of these students noticed the generic 'he' and said that it entered as a conscious factor into their decision to respond 'not apply.'*"[25]

Here are three of those responses:

— I said "not apply," because it was a lady. The "he" didn't agree. (Male)
— I said "not apply," because I expected a male and that's a female. (Male)
— I said "not apply," because it's a "he" and I couldn't decide whether a "she" would be appropriate. There was a clash between my mental image and the word. It could apply because of "someone," and "he" could be for no particular gender. I still pushed "not apply" because it was a girl. (Female)[26]

This last comment seems particularly enlightening as to the thought processes of a person asked to make a complex decision. Even knowing that generic *he* is *supposed* to be neutral has not been internalized as a reality by this student.

Among those students who pushed the "apply" button, many seem to have been taught the generic *rule* rather than responding spontaneously: "I guess I'm just so used to seeing 'he' meaning 'one,' like in analytical English, that I let it go. Right after I answered, I realized it was a woman, but then I thought, 'Well, OK.' (Female)"[27]

In the "Discussion" portion of the paper, Martyna remarks that some defenders of the generic masculine might use her data as proof that it was "doing its generic duty quite well." (80 percent) Such a conclusion would be mistaken inasmuch as the "study was deliberately designed to facilitate the drawing of a generic interpretation."[28]

Our actual encounters with "he" rarely take place in a generic context as clear as that devised for this study. In the language perhaps most familiar to this student population, that of educational materials, the sex-specific "he" appears five to ten times for every generic "he". . . .[29]

One scholar whom Martyna cites considered "he" and "man" so restricted by context that she called them "pseudo-generics."[30] This is a word for grammarians to ponder—both prescriptivists and descriptivists. After more than two centuries of insistence upon *he* as the "unmarked," "unspecified," and "neutral" pronoun, 20 percent of a test group of college students rejected the rule. The only feature of the generic masculine that is truly consistent is its history as a cornerstone of "correctness" in grammars written by men. Without the bolstering (one is tempted to call it boosterism) in the grammars and textbooks, would we have slid wholeheartedly into Bodine's "singular *they*" by now? In light of Martyna's research, it seems quite possible.

E. B. White ignored both Martyna and Bodine when he updated *Elements of Style* in the late seventies. A form of "they" is still wrong after such pronouns as "everyone," "anybody," and "someone." A form of "he" is obligatory since "he or she" is "awkward." White's explanation dismisses any other solution:

> The use of *he* as pronoun for nouns embracing both genders is a simple, practical convention rooted in the beginnings of the English language. *He* has lost all suggestion of maleness in these circumstances. The word was unquestionably biased to begin with (the dominant male), but after hundreds of years it has become seemingly indispensable. It has no pejorative connotations; it is never incorrect.[31]

In another publication Martyna writes:

> Some would say that such [psychological] consequences are minor, since ambiguity is common in our language and creates nothing more than mild confusion. The specific/generic ambiguities of *he* and *man*, however, lead to far more than confusion. Examinations of the "he/man approach" to language have focused on the social and psychological significance of the generic masculine usage.[32]

For example,

> Marguerite Ritchie has surveyed the legal implications of the generic masculine as it appears in Canadian law, concluding that its ambiguity has allowed either generic or specific interpretations to be drawn, depending on the judge's personal prejudices and the climate of the times.[33]

South of the border there are also indications that the masculine pronoun has been used against women. Take the case of Susan B. Anthony, who cast a vote in 1872 in Rochester, New York. She was arrested for "knowingly, wrongfully, and unlawfully" voting in the election. She had deliberately put the law to the test to see if she was a citizen (as defined in the 14th Amendment, 1868) and a voter (as defined in the 15th, 1870). She was convicted and fined $100 but refused to pay in the hope that she could then appeal the decision to a higher court. However, she was denied this opportunity since her failure to pay the fine was simply ignored.

Between the election in 1872 and her trial in 1873, Anthony toured the state lecturing on women's rights, or lack thereof, and she said the following about pronouns and the law:

It is urged that the use of the masculine pronouns *he, his* and *him* in all the constitutions and laws, is proof that only men were meant to be included in their provisions. If you insist on this version of the letter of the law, we shall insist that you be consistent and accept the other horn of the dilemma, which would compel you to exempt women from taxation for the support of the government and from penalties for the violations of laws. There is no *she* or *her* in the tax laws, and this is equally true of all the criminal laws.

Take for example the civil rights laws, which I am charged with having violated; not only are all the pronouns in the masculine, but everybody knows that it was intended expressly to hinder the rebel men from voting. It reads, "If any person shall knowingly vote without *his* having a lawful right." It was precisely so with all the papers served on me—the United States marshal's warrant, the bail-bond, the petition for habeas corpus, the bill of indictment—not one of them had a feminine pronoun; but to make them applicable to me, *the clerk of the court prefixed an "s" to the "he" and made "her" out of "his" and "him;"* and I insist if government officials may thus manipulate the pronouns to tax, fine, imprison and hang women, it is their duty to thus change them in order to protect us in our right to vote.[34]

Why is it if *he* is considered generic that in 1872 the male pronouns were all changed to female in order to avoid any ambiguity in Anthony's case? If Anthony and Ritchie are right—that the masculine pronoun has been used both generically and specifically in order to discriminate against women—then Geraldine Ferraro should have been on her guard in 1984, for Article II, Section 1, of the Constitution reads as follows: "The executive power shall be vested in a President of the United States of America. *He* shall hold *his* office during the term of four years, and, together with the Vice-President, chosen for the same term. . . ."[35] I found no argument in the press against Ferraro's choice by Mondale as his running mate on the grounds that the constitutional *he* prevented her nomination. There seems to be no pronoun qualification in running for President or Vice President.

Susan B. Anthony tested the pronoun qualification for voting and lost. It is probably because the 14th Amendment—the foundation of civil rights, the amendment that is used so often because it contains the words "due process" and "equal protection of the laws"—also contains the first instance of the use of the word *male* in the Constitution:

Section 2.

Representatives shall be apportioned among the several states according to their respective numbers, counting the whole number of persons in each state, excluding Indians not taxed. But when the right to vote at any election for the choice of electors for President and Vice-President of the United States, representatives in Congress, the executive and judicial officers of a state, or the members of the legislature thereof, is denied to any of the *male* inhabitants of such state, being twenty-one years of age, and citizens of the United States, or in any way abridged, except for participation in rebellion, or other crime, the basis of representation therein shall be reduced in the proportion which the number of such *male* citizens shall bear to the whole number of *male* citizens twenty-one years of age in such state.[36]

There is nothing generic about *male*, and the assumption that all voters must be male was retained until ratification of the 19th Amendment in 1920:

Section 1. The right of citizens of the United States to vote shall not be denied or abridged by the United States or by any states on account of sex.
Section 2. The Congress shall have the power to enforce this article by appropriate legislation.[37]

Phyllis Schlafly has claimed that she approved of the 19th Amendment, but was against the 27th (ERA) because of Section 2, which (as in the 19th) gives the federal government the right to enforce it.[38] Other opponents of the ERA have said that women are sufficiently protected by the 14th Amendment, that there is no need for yet another amendment prohibiting infringement of rights on the basis of sex. Yet the 14th is the very one that contains the word *male* thereby implicitly denying that women were part of the electorate. Schlafly's emphasis on Section 2 of the Equal Rights Amendment scared women who feared loss of "protection" under state law through interference from the federal government. Such an argument goes beyond the scope of this book since each state has its own statutes concerning divorce, child custody, and property.

Before leaving the pronoun problem, with or without envy, we should take a look at the first person. Although most of the linguistic skirmishing has focused upon generic *he*, feminists have also reviewed the situation with respect to how they speak of themselves collectively. Simone de Beauvoir wrote in 1949: " . . . women do not say 'We,' except at some congress of feminists or similar formal demonstration; men say 'women,' and women use the same word in referring to themselves."[39] Her point is proof of her argument that men think of themselves as "Self " and women as "Other" and that women have internalized this male view so that they think of themselves as "Other" also. Women do not (wrote Beauvoir) band together like other oppressed groups—Jews, blacks, the proletariat—and proudly say "we." Instead, they use the third person, demonstrating that they consider themselves secondary, subordinate, and inessential (as well as inauthentic).

Beauvoir's book is a cornerstone of modern feminism; hence, her assertions about how women refer to themselves have been taken very seriously by women writers. One example of the current agonizing reappraisal is to be found in an introductory textbook for women's studies courses called *Women's Realities, Women's Choices* by the Hunter College Women's Studies Collective.[40] The preface explains how the book was conceived and put together over a period of years; it also addresses the pronoun problem directly and at some length:

> Throughout this book, we its authors use the pronoun "we" to refer to women everywhere, in any period of history. The choice requires an explanation and some personal history.
>
> We, the authors, originally decided to try to take the point of view of women, to speak for women as subjects (we) rather than as objects (them), to speak, that is, for all of "us." The device of the pronoun, using "women . . . we" rather than "women . . . they" appealed to us, so we tried using it.
>
> We immediately ran into difficulties. The device struck some readers as awkward and artificial: "we the authors" did not take part in the French Revolution or suffer the indignities of slavery; how could we presume to speak for all women? Was it not either disrespectful or silly to pretend to do so?
>
> We decided that the manuscript should be rewritten, using "they" to refer to women collectively and in the contexts we were describing, and "we" to refer only to us the authors.
>
> It was at this stage that the chapters were put together and that many of us authors saw the book as a whole for the first time. As we read it over, we realized what had been lost in relegating women, again, to the voiceless "they," the "other," where patriarchy has always tried to put all of us.
>
> After much re-thinking and lengthy discussion of fresh criticism and reactions from new readers, we the authors revised the perspectives of the book yet again, again trying to speak, however haltingly, for all women. We the authors do not presume for a minute to be able to do so. We are only a small number of women with restricted backgrounds and limited experiences. We are of course not pretending to be able to give

adequate voice to the experiences of all women. But the authors of this book together with all those who read it and teach with it may be quite a large number of women with more varied backgrounds. We hope that women can be encouraged to see the world from the point of view of *women*, from the point of view of all of *us*, from *our* perspective. We hope the device of identifying with whatever women are being discussed in this book will help in this shift of perspective.[41]

If this preface had been published in the mid-seventies, some male columnist would doubtless have made fun of it, as George F. Will ridiculed McGraw-Hill's nonsexist guidelines, as William F. Buckley sneered at those of the publisher Scott, Foresman, and as Stefan Kanfer attacked the whole concept of women interfering with the language in an article called "Sispeak: A Msguided Attempt to Change Herstory."[42] This last is a very witty title, but all three of these normally urbane authors appear more condescending than understanding of the language problems involved in women's new awareness of themselves as human beings. It seemed to embarrass them, and they offered a helping hand to the poor ladies so that they would not further disgrace themselves by meddling with English. But their helpfulness and comfort appear thoroughly hypocritical. By trivializing women's attempts to grope toward a more equitable language, they only drew attention to their own assumed status as judges and authorities. Sarcasm permeates their advice. If men are so logical, so reasonable, and ahysterical as we have been led to believe, we should expect a more objective statement, such as:

> Thinking about profound social change, conservatives always expect disaster, while revolutionaries confidently anticipate utopia. Both are wrong.

This logical, reasonable, one might say "classical," statement was made by a woman—Carolyn G. Heilbrun.[43] She has a wider audience under the pseudonym Amanda Cross, author of many delightful detective novels. One of them—*Death in a Tenured Position*—deals with sexist discrimination in faculty appointments at Harvard. (Heilbrun is Professor of English at Columbia.)

Mary Daly used the first-person plural pronoun in 1973, under the influence of Simone de Beauvoir, for the following appeared two paragraphs after a reference to woman as "the Other":

Women may judge that in some cases the names imposed upon reality by male-dominated society and sanctified by religion are basically oppressive and must be rejected. In other instances, it may be that partial truth has been taken for the whole in the past, and that the symbols and conceptualizations that are biased have to be liberated from their partiality. Women will free traditions, thought, and customs only by hearing each other and thus making it possible to speak *our* word.[44]

5

Names and Titles

In 1973 Mary Daly wrote that

> Women have had the power of *naming* stolen from us. We have not been free to use our own power to name ourselves, the world, or God. The old naming was not the product of dialogue—a fact inadvertently admitted in the Genesis story of Adam's naming the animals and the woman.[1]

From the theological point of view, this may be true, yet women have probably always had something to say about the naming of their children, and more recently some have asserted authority over their own last names, choosing to keep their maiden names after marriage.* This option is not a product of the women's movement. Elizabeth Taylor, so far as I can tell, has never changed her name to that of any of her husbands', but that makes sense inasmuch as she was famous from the time that "National Velvet" was released—well before her first marriage.

To maintain one's maiden name, it is argued by militants, is to perpetuate patriarchal institutions. Why keep your father's name in protest against assuming some other man's name? (Those who keep their "maiden" names have altered their perception of the process by calling them their "birth" names—a valuable and accurate redefinition.) A middle road seems to be in hyphenation, but women who have

*Geraldine Ferraro became Mrs. John Zaccaro and then legally regained custody of her maiden name for professional purposes though remaining, in fact, Mrs. Zaccaro.

made this decision say it is not always convenient, especially if their maiden name and their husband's surname are both polysyllabic. One frequently encounters a couple whose wife's last name is hyphenated and whose husband's is not; their children often bear the mother's hyphenated surname. In case of divorce the names may or may not change, depending upon the mother's wish and the laws of the state in which she lives.

Even before women took to hyphenation or retention of maiden names after marriage I learned not to assume that a child's last name was also his mother's or father's. If one of my sons brought home a boy whose name was John Jones, I naively asssumed that he was the son of Mr. and Mrs. Jones and was proven wrong so frequently that I reversed my strategy: John Jones's mother or father probably did not bear the name Jones; and if I wanted to know where my son was when he went to play with Johnny, I had to collect the data in advance for our Rolodex. The phone book yielded scant information; the data were there in the white pages, but I found that I had a retrieval problem. Thus, the Rolodex grew with names and addresses not because I was afraid of making a social gaffe but simply to keep tabs on where my children were. The early Rolodex entries show mostly children whose parents were divorced and often remarried plus some children whose parents were living together without benefit of clergy or were living apart without benefit of clergy.

Then came hyphenation. The permutations grew: the main thing was to have addresses and phone numbers where these children could be located. My problem was geographical rather than strictly onomastic, and I noted that the children themselves seemed perfectly at ease with any last name they bore, whether it coincided with their mother's, father's, siblings', grandparents', or none of these.

Genealogists may find divorce and subsequent remarriage a stumbling block to their research, particularly where women have taken hyphenated last names but their husbands have not. The real trendsetter among linguists, who will drive future genealogists to apoplexy, is Cheris Kramer. Robin Lakoff referred to her under this name in *Language and Woman's Place* (1975) because Kramer's article in *Psychology Today* ("Folk-Linguistics: Wishy-Washy Mommy Talk," 1974) appeared under this by-line. But some time in 1978 Cheris Kramer became Cheris Kramarae. The explanation can be found in the preface to her book *Women and Men Speaking:*

At the time I married in Ohio, the state laws did not allow a married woman to legally retain her own name. So my name became, at the direction of the state, Cheris Rae Kramer. My middle name was the same as that chosen by my mother for herself when she left home for college. Now that state laws allow married women to name themselves independently of their husbands, and I am able to legally change my name according to my own wishes and directions, I have reordered the sounds to Cheris Kramarae.[2]

It would appear from the above that "Rae" was not Kramer's maiden name, nor even necessarily her mother's maiden name. Nevertheless, her decision as to how to rename herself could be a model for others. Practical and professional considerations obviously played a part: her surname had been "Kramer" since 1960 (the date of her marriage). By the time the laws of the state of Ohio changed, she had become well known in the profession as Cheris Kramer. If she had wanted to make a radical statement, she might have followed Judy Chicago—taking the name of her place of residence as a new last name—Cheris Urbana, or better yet, Cheris Champaign. Since Cheris is pronounced Sheris, her first and last names would have alliterated pleasantly. Still more radical would have been abandonment of both first and last names, an example set by Sojourner Truth in the nineteenth century. This sort of renaming is not necessarily done for political reasons, however. Writers often assume one or more pseudonyms, especially if they write different sorts of fiction. Even scholars have done this if they want to keep their own name for their "serious" work and a *nom de plume* for their novels (e.g., Carolyn G. Heilburn/Amanda Cross). Kramer's situation was not this complicated, and she wanted to maintain enough continuity between her "old" name and the "new," so she simply incorporated her middle name, "reordering the sounds," as she says.

Two features of her new last name are of special interest to the sociolinguist: (1) She put her own name *after* her husband's and (2) she merged them into one. Most married women who do not simply adopt their husband's surname add the husband's name at the end, usually (but not always) attaching it to their own with a hyphen so that the two are clearly distinct. To put one's own name after one's husband's seems to fly in the face of chronology and even history. In our linear, left-to-right graphic system, that which appears to the right is perceived as *later* than what precedes it. But the laws of the state of Ohio had denied Kramer's right to become anything but "Mrs. Kramer"; her recent conversion to "Kramarae" is thoughtful, practical, and esthetically pleasing. The phonetic and graphic merger of her own name with her husband's symbolizes a marriage of equals rather than the usual onomastic death of the wife—to my mind an ingenious answer to the question that is being increasingly asked by many women as they contemplate marriage.

When Kramer decided to make this change, she was bombarded with a variety of opinions, so much so that she says in her book she wished she had carried a tape recorder to document the suggestions she received (some from university and government officials). When she lectured about the subject of women and proper names, she found a great deal of interest in the topic. On the other hand, some thought "self-naming" was a joke.

> And some people, who hear nothing strange in giving all children the surname of only their father and giving wives the surname of their husbands, think that the disruption of a system of patronymic naming is quite wrong; or senseless. Several people shrugged their shoulders and said, 'Well, it's your name.' And I replied, 'Exactly.'[3]

Moreover, she seems to have incorporated a metronymic, i.e., a name derived from her mother, a third feature of her "self-naming" that demonstrates both innovation and continuity as well as a feminist stance.

In addition to proper names women have also insisted upon exercising the power to invent common nouns. Mary Daly called women's "new hearing and naming . . . cosmic upheaval. . . .Feminist naming is a deliberate confrontation with language structures of our heritage." She calls sexist language "the deafening noise . . . that has kept us from hearing our own word."[4] The theme of taking control of the language pervades her book. Since language has been used as a tool of oppression, it must be seized like a sword and wielded by women in their own defense. Her position contrasts sharply with Lakoff's, who wrote that language must follow, not precede, social change.

Daly wrestles with the problem of language explicitly, at times acknowledging that the perfect word with which to exercise "the power of naming" is not there. She must make do with what is already at hand, for example, the word "caste" to describe woman's position:

> The bonding [of women] is born out of shared recognition that there

exists a worldwide phenomenon of sexual caste, basically the same whether one lives in Saudi Arabia or in Sweden. This planetary sexual caste system involves birth-ascribed hierarchically ordered groups whose members have unequal access to goods, services, and prestige and to physical and mental well-being.[5]

She goes on to explain that she is not using the word "caste" in the narrowest sense, which would apply only to Brahmanic Indian society. "Our language at present lacks other terms to describe systems of rigid social stratification analogous to the Indian system." She adds that those who quibble over the use of the word "caste" to describe women's position probably do so in order to resist the insights that might derive from such a comparison. *Such rigidity overlooks the fact that language develops and changes in the course of history. The term is the most accurate available.*"[6]

Clearly Daly does not write "msguided sispeak." Rather than creating neologisms, she uses the traditional language while forcing it to do her bidding by making qualifications about the meanings of words that need discussion in order for their connotations to become clear. Her speculations about women's proper voice are instructive:

> It would be a mistake to imagine that the new speech of women can be equated simply with women speaking men's words. What is happening is that women are really *hearing* ourselves and each other, and out of this supportive hearing emerge *new words.*[7]

She rejects recourse to neologisms as the solution, however:

> This is not to say necessarily that an entirely different set of words is coming into being full blown in the *material* sense—that is, different sounds or combinations of letters on paper. Rather, words which, materially speaking, are identical with the old become new in a semantic context that arises from qualitatively new experience.[8]

Daly evidently found this linguistic approach inadequate, infusing old nouns with new meaning. She altered this position in two subsequent books—*Gyn/Ecology: The Metaethics of Radical Feminism* (Boston: Beacon Press, 1978) and *Pure Lust: Elemental Feminist Philosophy* (Boston: Beacon Press, 1984).[9] In the latter she describes herself on the book jacket as a "Nag-Gnostic," a new noun that almost makes her a heretic in the theological sense. "Gnostic" means "knower" or "believer," as opposed to "a-gnostic," an "unknower" or "unbeliever," but the Gnostics of early Christian times were heretics in the eyes of the Roman Catholic Church. Her linguistic playfulness and wit are radical only because her message is serious. A poet of light verse could get away with an invention like "Nag-Gnostic"; had it been created by Ogden Nash, he would have been praised for his verbal agility. A theologian trampling in such vineyards can scarcely escape criticism or at least raised eyebrows.

Mary Daly's approach to language differs from Lakoff's. Whereas Lakoff said that social change must pave the way for language innovation, Daly uses language as a reflection of female oppression and as a weapon whether men are ready to listen or not. She is not afraid of being labeled a "female castrator," whereas Lakoff urged women to stop their linguistic meddling lest men conclude that the female of the species is indeed irrational.

Daly has no such compunction: language must be transformed if patriarchal values are to be transvaluated, which would indicate that her assumption is that language paves the way to a new ethics. Language and feminism develop almost but not quite simultaneously; new language must be forged to express new ideas. Therefore, language has an effect upon reality. A similar idea is to be found in the work of Naomi Scheman, a philosopher engaged in reevaluating our understanding of the emotions. In her article "Anger and the Politics of Naming," she writes:

> The bestowing or the withholding of a name can be personally and politically explosive. To see that some state of affairs counts as oppression or exploitation, or that one's own feelings count as dissatisfaction or anger *is already to change the nature of that situation or those feelings.*[10]

Feminists have attacked various titles as being sexist, none perhaps with as much fervor as "Miss" and "Mrs." for their revelation of marital status, as opposed to "Mr.," which conceals it. The invention of "Ms." has solved this problem, or at least provided an option for those who wish to use it, though millions of women still prefer "Miss" or "Mrs." Other titles have been assaulted but without the same tenacity.

If we were still under British rule, we might be arguing about royal titles. "Were we their subjects," wrote Emily Post, "we would address them in the third person. But since this form of speech is not used by us, we are not considered discourteous when we say 'you.'"[11] Well, that's a relief. But should you be introduced to a royal prince, address him as "Sir" and a princess as "Ma'am" (not Madam), believe it or not.[12] Post devoted an interesting paragraph to the Duke and Duchess of Windsor, since they illustrated the problem of address when a royal prince (in this case a king who had abdicated the throne) marries a commoner (Wallis Warfield Simpson was an American citizen before she married the duke).

> When a royal prince or princess marries one who is not of royal birth, neither the wife nor the husband is accorded thereby the title of Royal Highness. For example, countless Americans have been introduced to the Duke and Duchess of Windsor. He of course is addressed formally "Your Royal Highness" and addressed by those who meet him socially as "Sir." The Duchess is addressed "Your Grace" by those who serve her, and by her friends as "Duchess," but never "Royal Highness" or "Ma'am." Together they are listed as His Royal Highness the Duke and Her Grace the Duchess of Windsor.[13]

Had you been faced with the prospect of entertaining such a couple, you should have given up your hostess's chair at the head of the table to the duke, and have seated yourself to his right. You should have put the duchess to your right, which is automatically the place of the guest of honor. By contrast to the above, arguments about "Ms." appear relatively uncomplicated.

That we still use titles at all is proof that Americans do have a sense of decorum, despite what Europeans may think to the contrary. We did not supplant "Mr.," "Miss," and "Mrs." by "Citizen" or "Comrade" after the Revolution, and Americans have as much intuition about the distinction between formal and informal usage as any other society. Although we move to first-name basis with a rapidity that foreigners often find alarming, we cling to "Mr." and "Miss," "Mrs." and/or the new "Ms." where the occasion calls for them, both in speaking and in writing. These titles are considered signs of courtesy, a medieval concept that derives from courtly procedures but which is by no means appropriate only for societies where monarchy has been retained. Part II of Robin Lakoff's *Language and Woman's Place*, entitled "Why Women Are Ladies," focuses on politeness (real and spurious) and will be discussed in the context of VII, "The Language Gene."

Let us for the moment assume that titles are not going to disappear immediately. It is possible to do without them, of course. I have received mail addressed to Alette Hill instead of "Mrs.," "Ms.," "Dr.," or

"Professor." The envelope doesn't bother me too much, nor my bare name on the inside over my address. The salutation "Dear Alette Hill," however, annoys me. It is incongruous, neither formal nor informal, and I seldom react positively to the computerized pitch that follows. Abolition of all titles would seem to be the only way of quelling the arguments, pro and con, over "Ms." Against the odds "Ms." has become acceptable in both speech and writing though it has not driven out "Miss" and "Mrs." The commercial success of *Ms.* magazine has no doubt helped the title "Ms." gain entrance into our permanent vocabulary. Although some feminists have objected strenuously to the editorial decision to accept slick ads that display automobiles, alcohol, and perfume with female models in a supposedly sexist light, I believe Gloria Steinem thereby made a major contribution to the larger cause of feminism by providing a continuing forum for debate.

It is illuminating to review the anger that the title "Ms." stirred up not too long ago. One of the most irate critics was Michael Levin, a philosopher who teaches at CUNY-Brooklyn and who has published a book called *Metaphysics and the Mind-Body Problem* (Oxford: Oxford University Press, 1979). He is also the author of "Vs. Ms.," which originally appeared in 1977, an article that he revised because "the original short piece was pirated, reproduced, and widely distributed, without permission, by an irate feminist."[14] I thought he was joking, but he is deadly serious. He begins "Vs. Ms." with a martial metaphor: "Academia has proved to be the Maginot Line in the defense of good sense against the panzer regiments of Women's Liberation." Feminists are Nazis here; later on in the article they become Russian Communists, identified by the image of the hammer and sickle. Why he casts Women's Liberation as the enemy on the far right and the far left is not clear except that both are totalitarian. He continues his opening salvo:

> Being a citizen of the occupied territory behind it, I have become familiar . . . with one of the most disturbing manifestations of that movement's influence: the warping of language to suit the ideological line of the new feminism.[15]

Levin's argument should be compared with Ann Bodine's in "Androcentrism and Prescriptive Grammar," in which she contends that although prescriptive grammarians have accused feminists of trying to change the language, it is they who have ruthlessly repressed the use of "singular *they*" for some 250 years.

Levin decries "chairperson" and "chairs" as well as "he/she's" and "Ms." "Every memo contains such terms, tacit sermons on or boosts for feminism. *These ugly neologisms* have long since spread to the media."[16] I don't know whether to label his essay a jeremiad or a philippic, but the author finds "Women's Lib" a bunch of "bullies" who "are attacking their easiest target—language."[17] Leaving aside his emotionalism (the article should be read in its entirety to get the full flavor of his outrage), I would argue that language is not an easy target but certainly a worthwhile one. That he takes such a serious view of language is to his credit. A philosopher who does not consider language an issue worth arguing over is no philosopher at all. Levin's view is nearly apoplectic in its tone though he has managed to keep his temper under control to the extent that his message is clear. After attacking various concepts of "Women's Lib" (e.g., housekeeping = "prostitution"), he says:

> This effort to mutilate English under the banner of "de-sexing" language is altogether pernicious. Efforts to legislate linguistic change to conform to a special world view have the net effect of making us unendurably self-conscious about our own language. Such a state of mind is profoundly unsupportable.[18]

In what sense women are both "mutilating" the language and "legislating" change is not explicit, but his main point here is interesting: it is unendurable and insupportable to be self-conscious about language. The man doesn't like to think about what he is saying.

> Language is the vehicle of thought and in an important sense *we must be unconscious of our choice of words* if we are to express our thoughts. When we become entangled with decisions about how to speak, we lose contact with the reality our speech is directed to. Surely the most uncomfortable moments of life are marked precisely by the need to think what to say: emotional scenes, awkward first dates, diplomatic negotiations with the boss. When things go smoothly we don't think about what words to use. We don't "choose our words"—they come unprompted.[19]

He does not understand that it is the spontaneous unrehearsed sexism in our language that has made women ill. Until they could dare to articulate their feelings in a language that scarcely supported the effort, they were trapped. Levin is aware that language is a tool of both thought and social change, yet he wants to remain comfortable with his mother tongue, and women are forcing him to think about what he says. He seems to have no capacity to put himself in their shoes, to imagine what it must be like to live a life of lies and deceit not of one's making. He has no desire to see the world through a woman's eyes, though he readily admits that blacks and Jews have been held in contempt for no good reason.

> many beliefs about "human nature" have fallen by the wayside . . . blacks were once held to be subhuman . . . Jews were thought to be of subnormal intelligence, etc. However, these past aberrations are all instances of xenophobia, easily explicable in terms of cultural differences.[20]

Levin seems to be ignorant of history with this facile statement. Scholars who have studied the Holocaust have not been able to explain on the basis of xenophobia why thoroughly assimilated German Jews went to the gas chambers. But at least Levin grants the blacks and the Jews some basis for discontent. Women are different from blacks and Jews, however, even though they may be both or all three (that is, black, Jewish, and female). The thought never occurs to him.

Levin grants that language "reveals something about ourselves, that features of language reflect reality and our perceptions."[21] Yet he does not say who is included in the pronoun "our." Instead, he offers up what to him is "interesting to ponder"—inflected languages where nouns show gender—for example, classical Greek. He appears not to know that Old English was inflected and that nouns had gender. It is important to him that in classical Greek

> the neuter coincides with the masculine roughly four times as often as it coincides with the feminine—and where it coincides with the feminine it coincides with the masculine as well. *These presumably unintended features of language are the linguistic traces of ancient and perennial perceptions.*[22]

He gives no source for this bit of wisdom, though students of Indo-European languages have been writing about gender and its possible meaning for more than a century.[23] Granted, Greek is an Indo-European language, but so are Sanskrit, Latin, and English. Why not count the nouns of masculine, feminine, and neuter gender in Old English if everyone knows what gender "means"? This question must go unanswered since Levin gives us no rationale for his choice and no footnote to his statistical survey of Greek nouns. We must approach this piece of literature like the "New Critics" of the fifties, judging the logic of his argument on purely internal grounds.

The content boils down to a statement that the neuter nouns coincide more frequently with the masculine than with the feminine, and where they coincide with the feminine, they also coincide with the masculine. If we translate this into some sort of sociolinguistic message, it would be that the Greeks thought eunuchs were more nearly like men than like women. That, I dare say, is not what he was driving at. Rather, he would apparently have us think that the preponderance of neuter nouns that are also masculine shows that the ancient Greeks were deeply ingrained with an unconscious preference for males over females, that maleness was, in fact, superior to femaleness. That may well have been a trait of Greek society, but it cannot be deduced from the gender-switching of neuter nouns. In the Judeo-Christian tradition there is evidence of sexism not only in Greek authors but also in Hebrew authors. The Old Testament is as shot through with masculist assumptions as the New Testament, and the message of the Church Fathers, both Greek and Latin, is similarly inclined toward the subordination of women, since man was created by God the Father, whereas woman was produced from Adam's rib. The "ancient and perennial perceptions" that can be gleaned from "linguistic traces" such as gender-marking in nouns may be nil, but the fact that sexism is embedded in Indo-European languages can be read in the records of those languages. These texts reveal male sex bias even when translated into English. A knowledge of Indo-European linguistics is not required.*

Levin's main point is to persuade readers that the title "Ms." should be abolished. The reference to Greek nouns serves the purpose of showing that gender marking is unconscious or un-self-conscious, something that Levin demands of language in general. He insists that "Ms." interferes with the generation of the species:

---

*For an idea of the complexities in the field, Levin should have consulted, *inter alia, Ancient Indo-European Dialects: Proceedings of the Conference on Indo-European Linguistics Held at the University of California, Los Angeles, April 25-27, 1963,* ed. Henrik Birnbaum and Jaan Puhvel (Berkeley and Los Angeles: University of California Press, 1966), especially the first article, by Henry M. Hoenigswald, "Criteria for the Subgrouping of Languages," pp. 1-12. That might have deterred Levin from dabbling in "folk-linguistics," a term coined by Hoenigswald.

Evolution has selected bisexual intercourse as that reproductive method which best mixes fecundity with genetic variety. Under such a system one sex must be the aggressor, the other the acceptor. If neither aggressed nothing would happen. If both aggressed, either nothing *but* mating would go on, or, more likely, the similarily of mating behavior of the sexes would deprive members of one sex from pursuing members of the opposite sex rather than their own and the species would die out. In the human species Man is the aggressor and Woman the accepter [sic]. Hence a man has to know, when encountering a new female, if she is eligible for his overtures.[24]

Woman needs no such knowledge about a man's marital status "since she is not the one responsible for initiation." Levin seems to be totally unaware of the fact that women also initiate sexual encounters through "feminine wiles." His knowledge of the social scene is uproarious. Does he think that Big Daddy Evolution would let a human invention like a title stand between Himself and procreation? For that is what Levin's attack is all about. "The most important fact of human existence is that women can have children and men cannot."[25] "Ms." will supposedly slow down the dating/mating game, and women's main function, after all, is child-bearing. The only reason for not dismissing Levin as a late-blooming Freudian is that Freud at least asked, "What do women want?"

My final objection to "Vs. Ms." is that Levin brands the feminists' linguistic efforts as an "attempt to impose Newspeak, and the dangers of imposing Newspeak are patent."[26] I must agree with him on the danger of imposing Newspeak and his statement a few sentences farther on that "What is shaping Orwell's Oceania is not linguistic change, but the negative conditioning of speakers." But as I have said earlier, Newspeak and the negative conditioning it involves were in place long before Orwell invented the term. Language has been used to keep women subservient and complacent. Some women have created new words to deal with linguistic inequity, words like "Chair" and "Ms." But even when women have not employed neologisms, they have been criticized if they attacked the subject of sexism before it became respectable. Simone de Beauvoir, Betty Friedan, and Kate Millett have been scorned and ridiculed for their ideas even though they wrote in a traditional manner. The ideas in their books are profoundly disturbing and were meant to be. That Mary Daly used the pronoun "we" instead of "they" broke the linguistic ice, as it were, although that option had been open to women all along. Simone de Beauvoir pointed out this fact in 1949, the year that *Nineteen Eighty-Four* was published.

L. M. Purdy wrote a response to Levin's tirade called "Against 'Vs. Ms.,'" in which she points out that the use of "Miss/Mrs." reflects a world view just as "Ms." does: if language is neutral, there is no harm in the use of "Ms."; if language is not neutral, then it is absurd to object to "Ms." while embracing "Miss/Mrs." as innocuous.[27] She further objects to his description of the mating game.

> We might ask why encounters must be characterized in terms of aggression. Perhaps this is the proper way to talk about encounters between rats and tigers, but men and women can and sometimes do behave in civilized ways, with expressions of interest replacing aggressions.[28]

She is not persuaded by the logic of Levin's argument any more than I am, and she destroys it systematically without even alluding to his dubious use of the gender-marking of Greek nouns. "To focus as exclusively as Levin does on women's purely biological possibilities at the expense of their intellectual and psychological ones is to imply that women have more in common with other species (like rats or cockroaches) than with men."[29] An eloquent rebuttal.

Another contributor to the same volume also takes issue with Levin's article but at greater length than does Purdy. Alan Soble divides "Vs. Ms." into four separate arguments, which he calls the "(1) *male sexual aggression*, (2) *female childbearing*, (3) *ideological introduction*, and (4) *spontaneity* arguments."[30] It would not seem to be necessary to deal with (1) and (2) at all, but Soble does so with elegance and determination. With regard to (1) he breaks it down further into five arguments and proceeds to demolish them. In the course of this demolition he makes the following observations: "The big flaw in Levin's argument is that he never explicitly defines what it means to be sexually aggressive or passive. . . . That Levin overlooks the many ways in which women have always been sexually aggressive . . . implies that he has become stuck in a world-view permeated more by ideology and wishful-thinking than by careful (even offhand) observation."[31] So much for *male sexual aggression*.

On point (2) *female childbearing*, Soble is equally relentless. Feminists have rejected the notion that women's most important function is childbearing. Nonfeminists should read Soble's discussion as to why

Levin's statement is not necessarily true, especially how Levin's "Miss/Mrs." convention

> restricts women to *one* (legitimate) category. The existence of two words conceals the underlying principle that dictates that women have only one status. . . . A "Miss" is merely not yet a "Mrs.," but is eligible to become one. To be a "Miss" is to be living in a no-woman's land, in limbo, awaiting the day when the title "Mrs." can finally be conferred.[32]

There is a paradox in the "Miss/Mrs." labeling, which Soble points out schematically. These titles send up a "smokescreen which barely conceals the fact that a woman has only one legitimate status."

Argument number (3) *ideological introduction* is then dealt with. Levin wrote that if "Ms." had been introduced without trailing clouds of ideology, he would have accepted it. Since it has been tainted by militant feminism, it is unacceptable. Soble says that if the title "Ms." were used only by women committed to the cause, then that would be an argument in favor of its retention and promotion by feminists. In this connection, he compares "Ms." with the word "black." "In the 1960s, to use 'black' instead of 'colored' or 'Negro' was to indicate that one was thoroughly in favor of civil rights for blacks, and often much more than this—black Nationalism."[33] However, the use of "black" is now standard. "To a certain extent this trend with 'black' and 'Ms.' is a healthy reflection that social movements have had some good effects on our linguistic habits and beliefs."[34] This statement sounds like Lakoff: social movements affect language, not the other way round. She said that the ground had already been prepared for the acceptance of the word "black," whereas at the time of her writing *Language and Woman's Place* (1975) she had never heard "Ms." used colloquially. Compare this with Soble:

> Of course, it is also unhealthy to the extent that the words have been used too loosely and have been stripped of their emotive and persuasive meanings. What this means, simply, is that linguistic change cannot be the only or even a basic technique used by social movements to generate change. But this is not to deny that linguistic change can be a helpful part of a program of social change.[35]

Soble and Lakoff sound alike on the importance of timing in the introduction of a neologism during a social revolution: early on, the use of a new word will announce the speaker as a revolutionary (Soble on "black"). If a word is generated too early, it may be restricted as to usage (Lakoff on "Ms."). Once over the hump of social change, the new word enters everyone's language though the early flavor of the word is lost (Soble on both "black" and "Ms."). Soble believes that linguistic change can be helpful in social change but not "the only or even a basic technique." By inference I assume that Lakoff would agree: if "Ms." really catches on in conversation, we will know that feminism has made inroads in society, but by implication the whole message of *Language and Woman's Place* is to persuade women that it is not in their best interests to speak like children. To stop speaking like a "lady," with all that the word bore in the way of connotations for Lakoff, was to begin to speak like an autonomous human being. There is just as much acknowledgment of the importance of linguistic change for social change in Lakoff as there is in Soble.

Before a woman can drop her speech patterns (stop using empty adjectives, changing the question intonation of many sentences to affirmative, and so on) and begin to speak authoritatively or at least assertively, she must switch mental gears, determine to alter a lifelong pattern, and do so consciously. That brings us to the last of Levin's four arguments against "Ms.," what Soble calls the argument from *spontaneity.* Soble is not sympathetic with Levin's assertion that "we must be unconscious of our own choices of words if we are to express our thoughts." Soble does not believe that "linguistic change will undermine the smoothness of thought and communication with language." He declares that although one may feel "awkward" when one first uses "he or she," even if one hesitates or stutters, the new usage becomes "nonconscious" after a week or so.

> The habit takes a surprisingly short amount of time to establish, with a wonderful effect on students who see and hear in action a successful move to overcome one's own conditioning (think about carrying out the linguistic change during a course of lectures on free will). Thus we can agree with Levin that our choice of words should be spontaneous, and yet disagree that it is impossible or tedious to change one's linguistic habits. Old dogs can teach themselves new tricks.[36]

Soble reveals himself ready to have a linguistic adventure in a good cause. He didn't have to change his entire approach to life, after all, and the discomfort he felt was not sufficiently great to discourage him. If a "lady" read *Language and Woman's Place* the year it was published, however, she would have to think long and hard about changing her linguistic patterns. If she decided that she was using any or all of the nine distinctive traits of "women's language" and wanted to drop them, she would have to make a conscious choice to sound like a "Self" rather than an "Other." Her new style of speech would probably produce extreme discomfort at first, especially if those around her perceived it as "bitchy" or uncooperative compared with her "old" self. Millions of women did just that in the years since Lakoff's book. Otherwise, we wouldn't be hearing so many women who were already grown up in 1975 speaking assertively. The "women's language" described by Lakoff can still be heard, but it does not appear to be the dominant style any more.

That male observers would have varying views on the subject of demands for linguistic equity should come as no surprise. Levin's argument for the preservation of spontaneity is altogether human. Why he should find innovation so uncomfortable to deal with, however, is idiosyncratic on his part. At any rate, Soble argues the point that spontaneity is not necessarily good in and of itself. It depends upon the circumstances whether one will find a totally unrehearsed and spontaneous style appropriate. In the free association of Freudian analysis it works; in diplomatic relations it does not. For the latter, one should weigh one's words very carefully. Moreoever, says Soble, Levin's argument from spontaneity is confused: where he takes the feminists to task for talking of housewifery as prostitution (for example), he is attacking metaphor—a redescription of reality rather than a change of language.[37]

> Despite the fact that Levin himself uses metaphor, it is quite understandable why he would fault the feminists for doing so. The conservative impulse behind the objection to "Ms." and in support of the traditional "Miss/Mrs." convention is the same impulse that shies away from any change, be it social or linguistic. Except, of course, change that reestablishes the wisdom of earlier times.[38]

So ends "Beyond the Miserable Vision of 'Vs. Ms.'"—a tour de force of critical acumen.

In a decade or even less, "Ms." became entrenched in the language. Notice the way in which Joseph Wambaugh uses it in dialogue (homicide detective to attractive secretary at Cal Tech, who wears no wedding ring):

> "Now we've got a problem, Miss Luna . . . is it Mrs. Luna?"

"It's *Ms.* Luna," she said, dashing his hopes, "but you can call me
Lupe."
That restored them a bit.[39]

Notice how deftly Ms. Luna keeps the detective at arm's length for a
few seconds with her title and then moves smoothly on to first-name
basis, which has the desired effect: the man is not discouraged from
pursuing her. If Levin was worried about the dampening effect of
"Ms." on the dating game, he should be reassured. Note too that Lupe
Luna is not wearing a wedding ring, a nonverbal sign that Levin does
not discuss. It turns out that she is the divorced mother of a fourteen-
year-old daughter. Whether Luna is her married or maiden name is
not revealed, nor is it pertinent; what *is* significant is that Lupe Luna
chose to conceal her marital status and to rebuff the detective initially
but not so forcefully that he would give up altogether. Therefore her
use of "Ms." can be seen as assertive speech but not as a badge of man-
hating or condescension.

By insisting on "Ms." a woman signals that she is self-respecting.
Therefore, the language that a man uses on her should be respectful.
It is a request for reciprocity and mutuality. If the detective were put
off by the title "Ms.," he could simply retreat, as Levin says is inevita-
ble. The detective does not do this; "Ms." merely provides him an instant clue as to what kind of woman Ms. Luna is—an independent
grownup. Despite the "ideological clouds" that heralded the appearance of the title, it seems to have weathered the storm of conservative
protest and ensconced itself as an option for women who feel that neither "Miss" nor "Mrs." is appropriate and/or that it is not necessary to
announce one's marital status with one's name. This small step toward parity irritated and enraged many people besides Michael
Levin. The reason would seem to be that they felt "Ms." was only the
beginning, the tip of the iceberg; there would be endless demands for
linguistic change. "Ms." & Co. have not been so catastrophic as predicted.

What then is the cultural meaning of "Ms."? Here is one answer:

Feminist discourse has suggested both negative and positive implications
of language in women's lives. Language, many claim, plays a crucial role
in defining and maintaining a "man's world" while delineating and en-
closing "women's place." In trying to move beyond that confining place,
many women are attending to and changing the verbal realities of their
daily lives. Women across America are adopting the new title *Ms.*, affirm-

ing independent identities through name choices and changes, protest-
ing a perpetual "girlhood" verbally conferred, and supporting one
another in "speaking up."[40]

William Safire has now given his stamp of approval to "Ms." In an
astonishing though grudging move to the left, Safire decided that this
was the only appropriate title for Geraldine Ferraro.[41] Since some
newspapers and magazines will not print "Ms." (I didn't know this, but
Safire works for one—*The New York Times),* Ferraro chose "Mrs." as
better than "Miss" since it labeled her as married. Safire argues that
she is not Mrs. Ferraro; that's her mother's name. She is Mrs. Zaccaro. "She has her choice of being known as Miss Ferraro or Mrs. Zaccaro, but not—to my way of thinking—as 'Mrs.' Ferraro, a person she
is not."[42] Then Safire gets hot under the collar.

> It's one thing to be deferential to feminists' wishes; it is another to twist
> the meaning of words to accommodate any political leader's desire to
> style herself any way she likes. If Mrs. Zaccaro or Miss Ferraro can be
> called "Mrs. Ferraro," why can't her opponent, Mr. Bush, ask to be called
> "Mr. Lincoln"? What if he asked to be called "Mrs. Bush"? Would news-
> papers refuse him the honorific he might prefer in this admittedly outra-
> geous example just because he is not Mrs. Bush? Miss Ferraro is not Mrs.
> Ferraro, yet she gets the honorific she prefers.[43]

After this inane though amusing argument, Safire stops frothing at
the mouth, reconnoiters, and states the case fairly:

> That's not quite accurate: the honorific she prefers is "Ms.," and the
> "Mrs." is to her the lesser evil than to appear in a photo with her husband
> and three children with the caption identifying her as "Miss," which does
> not quite fit in with traditional family values.

Lord be praised. The man is honest. And now for the belated though
welcome male seal of approval:

> It breaks my heart to suggest this, but the time has come for "Ms." We
> are no longer faced with a theory, but a condition. It is unacceptable for
> journalists to dictate to a candidate that she call herself "Miss" or else use
> her married name; it is equally unacceptable for a candidate to demand
> that newspapers print a blatant inaccuracy by applying a married honor-
> ific to a maiden name.[44]

Now this is a linguistic victory of the first order. Although broken-
hearted, a columnist whose beat is language has decided after much

soul-searching that "Ms." has a place in our Mother Tongue. He is not happy with it, but he is less happy with inaccuracy. Moreover, he calls "Ms." as "fuzzy" as "Mr."—a title that conceals a man's marital status. He could have proposed two titles for men—one for bachelors and one for married men (something Russell Baker suggested facetiously as a way of squashing "Ms." early on), but he doesn't and it's easy to see why when you read the end of the column, which was written by the editors of *The New York Times* in rebuttal:

> Some days the Title Question appears to claim more time—and ignite more passion—than the East-West arms race.
> We accept anyone's choice—in this case, Geraldine Ferraro's choice—of a professional name. But a title is not part of the name. Publications vary in tone, and the titles they affix will differ accordingly. The Times clings to traditional ones ("Mrs.," "Miss" and "Dr.," for example). As for "Ms."—that useful business-letter coinage—we reconsider it from time to time; to our ear, it still sounds too contrived for news writing.[45]

One can see why Safire did not revise the "fuzzy" title "Mr." with two new alternatives: the august editors of *The New York Times* do not use nontraditional titles. End of discussion. Our great liberal newspaper of record in the largest city in the land publishes all the news that's fit to print but not all that's new, and to their collective ear, "Ms." is obviously unfit. Safire's argument on the grounds of accuracy does not impress them: they would rather be wrong than nontraditional. How long, one wonders, will "Ms." have to wait in the antechambers until *The New York Times* grants a favorable audience?

Though "Ms." is now in the dictionary and in daily conversation, the editors consign it to business correspondence only. Their explanation is based on two facts: (1) it is contrived and (2) it hurts their "ear." One cannot argue with either. The first is certainly true, but do the editors disallow "black" on the same grounds? No. But then "black" is not a title, nor is it as "contrived" as "Ms." The second excuse is a personal reaction derived from esthetics. They could turn a deaf ear to any title, or any word for that matter, that offended it.

Note that the vice-presidential candidate preferred "Ms." By refusing to employ this title, *The New York Times* offered a choice of "Mrs." or "Miss," and her decision in favor of "Mrs." caused an error that Safire first attacked in his column, a tactic called "blaming the victim." Upon reflection, even he saw the injustice of his rebuke and was moved to support "Ms." His bosses, however, remained implacable. Their condescending and blasé rebuttal shows what they think of women and their trivial requests, not in a league with "real" news like the East-West arms race. *The New York Times,* by its own admission, is not a newspaper at all but an oldpaper.

Now that *The Times* has printed "Ms." and "Ms. Ferraro," its pure reputation has been sullied. It is no longer a virgin, so to speak, and might as well give up its fight to protect its mysterious "ear." Seduced by its columnist into printing the offensive two-letter obscenity, it cannot go back to its former policy with a clean record. Many women will find *The Times*'s rebuttal chauvinistic and not at all persuasive, for its editors proudly reveal their boredom with the "Title Question." Women may have the title of their choice, so long as it's "Mrs." or "Miss."

6

Terms of Endearment

Terms of endearment are words used by close friends, families, and lovers, or so one would think, but they are also used on women by perfect strangers. This usage constitutes another example of nonparallel construction, one that demonstrates a double standard and supplies further evidence for discrimination based on sex.

I would have thought that this phenomenon was moribund, but only this year in a local restaurant the waitress addressed my husband as "Sir" and me as "dear." We were dressed in appropriately casual middle-class clothes for breakfast in a sedate but by no means fancy restaurant. I could not have been perceived as a daughter of a daddy or "sugar daddy" since my husband is only two years older than me. Why, then, should I be addressed as "dear," which I found insulting? The waitress must have assumed that I was flattered by her intimacy; she was hustling for a tip, telling us how delicious our omelettes looked and how fast the service was. The omelettes were fine; the service was slow (both compliments of the chef). I found the sales pitch crass and my chummy status as "dear" revolting. Perhaps the waitress had recently emigrated from a community where this is normal parlance. I could have whipped out my credit card to command some respect, but I controlled my urge to teach in public.

The "sir/dear" phenomenon is discussed by Nessa Wolfson and Jean Manes in "Don't 'Dear' Me!"—an article that surveys forms of address in what the authors call "service encounters."[1] Their rationale for doing extensive field work—800 "interactions," of which more than 80 percent were service encounters—is as follows:

There has been growing interest over the past few years in the way the use of language reflects women's status. All too many of the studies which focus on this issue have suffered from a lack of data from everyday conversational interactions, a problem which is not infrequent in studies of other aspects of language in society. However useful intuitions may be for suggesting hypotheses, it is only through empirical investigation that one may hope to ascertain the validity of one's suppositions. For this reason, it was essential to observe and record data from everyday linguistic interactions; in no other way could we obtain the information needed to analyze the factors which might be involved in the choice of specific address forms.[2]

Since it is essential for linguists on the track of real speech to keep the speakers in the dark about the fact that an experiment is in progress, the authors chose service encounters as the slice of life to investigate, for most people engage in such encounters every day. There was a vast area of opportunity for salespeople, waiters/waitresses, and clerks to reveal their ordinary parlance to strangers (the investigators).

Wolfson and Manes found three dominant modes of address for women: (1) "dear," (2) "ma'am," and (3) nothing (i.e., no form of address). "What is most significant . . . is the fact that each of the three can be shown to occur in functionally equivalent situations, to form, in effect, part of a paradigm."[3] They ask the reader to imagine all three in the setting: "Can I help you?" and assume that we (female shoppers) have indeed heard "dear" (or perhaps "hon"), "ma'am" (or sometimes "miss"), and zero ("Can I help you?" with nothing added). It seems anomalous that a term of endearment should correlate with a form of respect like "ma'am" in the same context.

The examples are many and varied, one revealing Lakoff's "women's language," though the authors don't make this connection.

> When one of the researchers called shoe stores in the Philadelphia area to ask whether they carried girls' saddle shoes, she received, among others, the following responses:
> (4) No, I'm positive we don't have them in stock.
> (5) No, I can't help you, ma'am.
> (6) *I don't believe we have them here, hon.*[4]

Their point is to demonstrate that "Whenever two or more forms can occur within the same frame with no change in referential meaning, their differential usage is likely to carry social meaning."[5]

The service frame may be loosely the "same" in (4), (5), and (6), but I detect a difference in style among the three excluding the form of address: (4) and (5) are assertive and straightforward, whereas (6) is less definite. "I don't believe . . . " is a hedge against the directness of a simple negation or denial, and (6) contains the endearment "hon." The hedge and the endearment belong together, the hedge softening the brusque edge of a simple "no" and the endearment serving to "cuddle" the customer, both ploys attempting to smooth over the harsh reality of not having in stock what the buyer wants. Number (4) with zero address form and (5) with respect form are considered more appropriate for a stranger than "hon," which might offend a customer by being too familiar, cozy, and perhaps presumptuous.

As the authors point out, a zero form (i.e., lack of address form altogether) may well strike most customers as the most polite or least offensive since not everyone likes to be called "ma'am." If the tone of voice is accommodating rather than abrupt, zero address is often the best choice; formal ("ma'am") is also acceptable to almost everyone; whereas informal ("dear," "hon") may be perceived as insincere, phony, or simply gauche (my adjectives; I am extrapolating from Wolfson and Manes here). If I am right, then it follows that the assertive language of (4) and (5) meshes with the address forms; in (6) there is also a perfect mesh, inasmuch as the hedge and the endearment both represent forms of ingratiation—a softening of the message ("no, we don't have what you want") plus "hon," to show that the salesperson "cares" about the customer as a "person." It would be enlightening to hear this woman outside the work place to see if she routinely speaks "women's language" (I wouldn't be at all surprised), but the authors have limited their experiment to service encounters for good reason.

Another significant feature of their report is that they cover two different regions—the northeast and the southeast. They found that although "ma'am" is used in both, "the frequency and distribution of the form show strong regional differences."[6] Southerners used "ma'am" 68.5 percent of the time, endearments 31.5 percent. Northeasterners used "ma'am" 24.5 percent of the time *and an endearment form 75.5 percent of the time.*"[7] This surprising proportion (almost an inverse ratio) between these contiguous areas is a clue to language customs in general and gives one a handle on the habitual misinterpretation of personality traits that baffle both Yankees and Southerners when dealing with each other both within and beyond the service encounter setting. In both cases the regional speech forms often strike the "foreigner" as hypocritical. Yankees exposed to the ubiquitous "ma'am" for the first time will frequently assume a phony veneer (reinforced by what seems to be a syrupy accent), while Southerners are confirmed in their stereotypical distrust of Yankees as crude hucksters by the widespread use of endearments on them by total strangers.

There are some uses of "ma'am" that are exclusive to the South, for example, in response to a question that the respondent didn't hear or understand.

(12) A: Could you tell me how late you're open this evening?
      B: Ma'am?
      A: Could you tell me how late you're open this evening?
      B: Until 6.

Here "ma'am" is equivalent to "pardon?" or "I'm sorry?" which are used both south and north of the Mason-Dixon Line.[8]

The second use of "ma'am" peculiar to the South carries the meaning "You're welcome."

(15) A: Could you tell me how late you're open this evening?
      B: Until nine.
      A: Thank you very much.
      B: Yes, ma'am.*

Wolfson and Manes tell the following anecdotes to illustrate Yankee culture shock at southern locutions:

> a male colleague of one of the researchers, who is a good deal older than she is and who generally addresses her by first name or a diminutive, responds to direct questions from her with "yes, ma'am," or "no, ma'am." *Even more striking to a transplanted northerner is a young man from South Carolina who, when his wife says something he does not hear, questions her with, "Ma'am?"*[9]

"Ma'am" is so commonly used in the South as to be virtually automatic and therefore not necessarily a gauge of respect. The authors quote

---

*In Colorado the native equivalent of "You're welcome" is "You bet," though "Yes, ma'am" can also be heard. "You bet" is also heard in other parts of the west. Unlike "ma'am" it is seldom used by women, whereas endearments are infrequently used by men who are not known to the speaker.

passages in which the informant used "ma'am" even though obviously annoyed by the speaker. Irritation is apparent by the informant's use of "lady" as well as "ma'am." "Lady," though the authors do not comment upon this word, is not a substitute for "ma'am"—quite the reverse. It is most often uttered sarcastically and can be heard in both the North and the South. Belligerent cab drivers have appropriated this anomalous use of the word "lady" (one not discussed by Lakoff, though it may well be used to support her contention that a "lady" is viewed by some men as a silly tiresome creature). Here are two examples that Wolfson and Manes offer to illustrate the fact that "ma'am" need not convey respect in the mouths of southern males. Note how the intercalated "lady" appears insulting, whereas "ma'am" can be construed as neutral:

(17) A: Mr. Jones?
      B: Yes, ma'am.
      A: I'm calling for Jim Smith, who's running in the Democratic primary next Tuesday.
      B: Yes, ma'am.
      A: May I ask what you think of Mr. Smith?
      B: I'll tell you, *lady.* I'm voting for Jim Brown.
      A: Well, thank you very much.
      B: Yes, ma'am.

and

(18) A: *Lady,* I've spent my whole morning down here waiting.
      B: Did you put your yellow card in the box?
      A: Yeah.
      B: (looks in the box and locates card) Did you want to get these filled out?
      A: Yes, ma'am.

Their comment on (18): "Other speakers may express their annoyance by avoiding the polite address form, switching back to it when they feel their grievance is being attended to. . . . "[10] A "grievance" may not have been dealt with in (17), but the switching back and forth between "ma'am" and "lady" reveals *annoyance* in both (17) and (18). "Lady," invariably showing annoyance or irritation, is not regionally confined. "Lady" contrasts sharply with "ma'am" in (17) and (18) but also with terms of endearment like "dear" and "hon," which the authors say co-occur with such speech acts as teasing, "which are typical of interactions between intimates."[11] Between strangers, however, terms of endearment imply a judgment of incompetence on the part of the target. Example (telephone interchange):

(29) A: Does the doctor have office hours tonight?
B: Yes, he does. He has hours from 7 p.m.
A: From 7 until when?
B: From 7 until he's done, hon.

In this case, the speaker does not shift to a generally less impersonal speech mode; rather she makes use of the term *hon* when answering what she sees as an unnecessary, and possibly even foolish, question.[12]

Another example involves a cashier at Woolworth's, a series of customers, and a co-worker. The first customer is addressed as "ma'am," the interrupting co-worker as "hon," and a second customer, who has added to her purchases and therefore needed another receipt, as "hon" twice—even though this second customer was a good bit older than the cashier. On the basis of these and other examples the authors generalize:

An examination of all instances of terms of endearment in our data shows that, when such a term is other than the standard address form for that speaker, its use is generally triggered by something in the interaction which shows the customer to be somewhat less than totally competent.[13]

Among intimates terms of endearment are applied reciprocally except when children are involved. Children do not call their parents or other grownups by the endearments used on them. So it is in service encounters: where terms of endearment are used, they are nonreciprocal. The authors think that the "meaning" of nonreciprocal use is the same: "the implication is that the speaker and addressee are not equals.[14] When the cashier switched from "ma'am" to "hon" during a service encounter, the customer was dependent upon the cashier, who was in control of the situation.

For this reason, the cashier, instead of using the respect form *ma'am*, uses a term which indicates precisely the *lack* of need for any expression of respect . . . [imposing] on the addressee a form which implies intimacy or lack of social distance in a situation which does not allow reciprocal usage, a behavior normally associated with interactions with children.[15]

The explanation of how a respect form like "ma'am" and a term of endearment like "dear" can be found in the same context shows the ambiguity in service encounters where perceptions of power govern address forms. It also explains why women—though showing no sign of helplessness or incompetence—can be called "dear" even when in the company of a man who is addressed as "sir"! The stereotype of the "lady" as childish and incompetent must be at the heart of these disparate usages. A woman is automatically subordinate just as children are subordinate, demonstrated by the speaker's use of "dear" and "hon," which though superficially friendly is, in fact, a sign of condescension and therefore a source of irritation to women who sense the discrepancy.[16]

The woman who feels like Wolfson and Manes—"Don't 'Dear' Me!"—is not paranoid. She is sensitive to nuances in the language that is spoken to her every day. Their research uncovers a linguistic double standard that persists despite women's new assertiveness, for the speakers who use terms of endearment on female customers do so spontaneously from long habit. Here is an example that Michael Levin might well consider when he insists that spontaneity and unconscious speech patterns are desirable. If he were "deared" and "honned" every day like a child or an incompetent adult, he might understand why women question his conviction that language must remain as it is for the sake of his comfort and that of other men.

A horrifying example of how terms of endearment can be used to put women in their place can be found in an exposé by a medical writer whose 85-year-old mother went into "one of America's best hospitals" for routine tests for painful legs. This woman, who was impeccably groomed and in total control of her mental faculties, turned into a pathetic victim when treated like an incompetent. The staff assumed that anyone 85 years of age was senile. They took away her comb, her dentures, and her eyeglasses as well as "misplacing" her lovely nightgown and robe. By the time the author was able to visit, her mother looked like a hag.[17]

A young orderly called her "Doll," "Grannie," and "Annie" (her first name was Anna). Since she was European by birth and upbringing, she was used to being called Anna only by her family and closest friends. The staff revealed their contempt for the elderly by calling her whatever they wished. After taking blood sample after blood sample, X ray after X ray, the physicians decided to perform a spinal tap and a bone marrow examination. In order to extract enough bone marrow, "they had to pierce her breastbone. She said it hurt terribly, but everybody told her, '*Old people's bones are so brittle. It can't hurt much. Be a good girl, Annie.*'"[18]

From this unbelievably callous treatment to her death two days later, the patient cowered in bed, cried whenever she saw anyone in a white coat, and lapsed into her native German. The neurologist who examined her took the daughter aside to inquire if there was a history of insanity in the family since the old lady was talking "gibberish"! Her daughter explained that her mother was not psychotic: she was speaking German. No apology was forthcoming.

After these painful and debilitating tests, the staff saw fit to subject the now terrified patient to the theater of the absurd: they rolled her into an auditorium to be poked and prodded (unkempt, unwashed, and terribly embarrassed) as a "teaching" subject for interns and residents, though she was in pain and totally exhausted. The daughter would have prevented this last outrage had she known it was planned, but she was not informed. Now the patient was demoralized and very ill as a result of her treatment. She was dizzy and had lost control of her bowels. It took a half hour to get a nurse's aide to change the sheets. The daughter concluded that the five elderly people on that floor were the last to get any service. "'Those people are always complaining' or 'They just want attention' were sentiments heard a lot around the nurses' station."[19] Her mother began to have difficulty breathing that evening, but the floor resident had ordered one more X ray. She objected as firmly as she could in German—"*Nein*" ("no"). The orderly replied. "'Now don't you be difficult, Dolly. . . .'" The patient then spoke in English to the young man, who was younger than her youngest grandson: "'My name is Mrs. Simon.'" Those were her last words; her heart stopped before they could wheel the gurney into the elevator.

Mrs. Simon's self-respect was assaulted both physically and psychologically by males and females alike. "Old" meant "senile" to the hospital staff. They used a diminutive of her first name—"Annie"—and what might pass for terms of endearment—"Doll," "Dolly," and "Grannie," which would seem to be geriatric variants of "hon" and "dear." Given the circumstances—Mrs. Simon's personal formality, her scrupulous attention to her appearance, her demonstrated independence for 85 years—these "endearments" can be seen as insults. If "hon" and "dear" are used on women because they are perceived as inferiors, they perhaps serve to elevate the user's ego and afford him or her a sense of importance. Just so the degradation of the elderly may reflect a cultural tendency (I'm tempted to go so far as to call it sadism) to dehumanize and demoralize the most vulnerable population in the land. This trend is but another example of blaming the victim.

Even in intimate relationships, terms of endearment are not necessarily used in a reciprocal fashion. Some men use "dear" and "darling" only when angry or irritated, that is, with a sarcastic tone of voice. It is quite possible to have an intimate relationship (with or without benefit of clergy) that is neither reciprocal nor mutual, where the man remains a Self and the woman, an Other. Although married women are no longer literally their husbands' property, as was the case in the nineteenth century, their subordinate position is still so widely assumed that names, titles, and terms of endearment reflect this disparity. Terms of endearment in intimate relationships, however, go far beyond the purview of "Don't 'Dear' Me!" A feminist would shun a man who treated her like a child or even as a subordinate, yet a woman who was married in the fifties or sixties and then had her consciousness raised might chafe under newly perceived slurs in the guise of endearments. Some men are no longer referring to their wives as "the ball and chain," but the permutations on this theme are virtually open-ended and not amenable to empirical testing.

That younger women no longer suffer fools gladly (or insults either) seems to be a safe generalization (all generalizations being subject to exceptions, of course). The prevalence of "living together" openly before or without marriage testifies to a nontraditional approach that no longer brands the woman involved with a scarlet A on her forehead. (Men were never so branded, of course.) Living together, unlike "keeping a mistress," implies a degree of reciprocity, and in its wake reveals a lacuna in the language: whereas a man may still refer to his "girlfriend" as just that, a woman feels awkward calling her "boyfriend" a boyfriend unless she is still a teenager.

Some light has now been shed on this subject by Stephanie Brush, author of *Men: An Owner's Manual,* a guide to modern cohabitation.[20] When asked by an interviewer, Cutler Durkee ("a practicing male"), "What should you call the man you live with?" Brush replied:

> Besides Al? Well, let's say your're at a party. You can introduce him as "My guy," but you sound like one of Martha and the Vandellas. Or you

can say, "This is my old man," but you sound like Grace Slick. Grace Slick 10 years ago. You can say, "This is my boyfriend," but everyone will think your parents are still waiting up for you in Fair Lawn, N. J.[21]

When Durkee suggested calling him "honeybunch," Brush was not enthusiastic. "I think people would throw up. You can also say, 'This is my lover,' but that only sounds plausible if his name is something like Xavier."[22]

Neither Brush nor Durkee has provided a good answer except "Al." Perhaps "Al" plus last name would suffice for formal occasions. We have come a long way from Emily Post, who did not deal with illicit liaisons. Although Brush's book is a humorous how-to manual, she provides a guide to the perplexed, i.e., useful information along with gags. Live-ins are neither gigolos nor mistresses; the arrangement is presumably reciprocal, but like marriage it often falls short of this liberated utopian vision. Since Brush has a career, she (and others in her circumstances) would not want to play Mommy to a hippie slob, but the interviewer turns the tables on this stereotype by asking, "How do you know if the man you're living with is excessively neat?" to which Brush replies, "There are several signs, but the most obvious is that there will be Airwick refills where most normal men keep their pornography."[23]

Emily Post, were she still alive, might be expected to succumb to an attack of the vapors about now. Brush's humor and light-heartedness are worlds away from *Etiquette: The Blue Book of Social Usage*. Post's manual was written for the haute bourgeoisie and for those who would emulate the Establishment. It is prescriptive in the extreme and loaded with tips on what not to do for fear of being considered a yokel. Brush starts from a descriptive base in a changing world. Though urban as well as urbane, she makes no attempt to intimidate her readers by references to the Right People and the In Places. She is bright and attractive and quite willing to change live-ins by mutual consent, but here is one piece of advice elicited by her inteviewer that shows where even liberated women have to curb their spontaneity. Durkee asks, "Do men appreciate funny women?" The reply sheds some light on Lakoff's remark that ladies are supposed to be humorless, neither telling nor "getting" jokes:

If you ever read the Bachelor of the Month column in *Cosmopolitan* you know that what men really want is "a woman with a sense of humor"—

and not just because it's very crude to say, "I go for giganto tits." But what you have to face is that a woman with a sense of humor isn't a woman who makes jokes, it's a woman who laughs at jokes. Let's say you just whipped off the greatest one-liner since Jack Benny went off radio. A man's gonna put his hands on his hips and say, "I see, so now we're getting *sarcastic*." If you catch yourself trying to be funny, *bag it*. Walk into the bathroom, lock the door and practice saying into the mirror over and over, "So these two flamingos walk into a bar . . . " until you get it out of your system.[24]

This vestige of male dominance dictating feigned female stupidity is disappointing. It is *disturbing*, in fact. If women are attractive to men only if they appreciate men's jokes, but practicing this art is the kiss of death, we have evidence that the dictum "man does, woman is" still rules. All those articles I read in *Seventeen* years ago counseling girls to play dumb and praise one's date for his brilliance (even if he's a fool) bring back painful memories, and although women may display technical know-how in medicine, law, politics, and even engineering, they must still apparently play adoring audience to the man's jester if they would be "popular."

Surely humor can't be threatening in the way that intelligence used to be? Upon reflection, though, I can see a connection, for wit implies *wits*. Must we remain geisha/Stepford wives (programmed for perfection by the male owners), smiling vacantly but never letting ourselves be funny? I hope not, but Brush's admonition is sobering. Jokes are still male turf; women who tell jokes are suspected of not knowing their place. People of the same caste can be safely humorous only among their peers. To say something even mildly outrageous when among the members of a higher caste is to risk ostracism. Here, as always, women are Others, while the men continue to be Selves. There is an air of sanctity and sacerdotal reverence: the High Priests (let alone The Unwashed) do not make jokes about the naked emperor or reveal that the Wizard of Oz is a fraud. Jokes about sacred personages might be construed as a sign that the natives are restless and "uppity."

When Erma Bombeck turned the feminine mystique into a farce, she drew a large audience of mostly female readers, for her column was aimed at the daily frustrations and unsung triumphs of housewife-mothers. Though her comments have grown somewhat bolder over the years to render her feminist point of view explicit, she is more popular than ever. Nevertheless (as mentioned earlier), she is still affronted by Betty Friedan's early reproach to humorous housewives. Bombeck remembers thinking, "God, lady, you can't make it better tonight. What more do you want from us? . . . first we had to laugh; the crying had to come later." (Notice the irritation in the use of "lady.") Other feminist recruits were turned off the program totally; Friedan's stern and largely humorless approach to the revolution appeared both unrealistic and unsympathetic. Yet Bombeck was working from the same data base—the world of the housewife-mother— and with the same assumption—women are people, too. It is paradoxical that to Friedan, housewife-writers were enemy agents offering the life jacket of laughter against the sea of suppression and one should not cultivate false friends ("Swim on your own, *lady*"); to Bombeck, laughter was necessary for survival ("Share mine, Mildred. What bra size do you wear anyway?")

Comedy can indeed be a support service, a flotation system for the drowning. Was everyone supposed to issue an ultimatum to her family and get a divorce if instant capitulation were not forthcoming? It was no doubt saner and more political to assume that women would remain loyal to husband and children no matter how high their new consciousness had been raised even if they now viewed marriage as a potential deathtrap for the psyche.

Robin Lakoff listed among her nine distinctive features of "women's language" the notion that ladies are not supposed to be able to tell or even "get" jokes. If that is part of the stereotype under which we have been laboring, then an outburst of laughter is a clue that a woman has rejected the Dumb Dora model. Lakoff does not provide an explanation as to why women are thought to be humorless, but one reason could be that humor indicates a lively intelligence and an irreverent attitude toward venerable institutions like patriarchy. If savvy Stephanie Brush believes that women should never tell a joke if they want to remain popular with men, we can be sure that wit is viewed as threatening by males; safer to play witless.

Yet there are funny women—Joan Rivers, Elaine May, Lily Tomlin, Jane Curtin, and Lorraine Newman, for example. There is also the brilliant Fran Lebowitz, who seems to hold nothing sacred except linguine with clam sauce. On childraising, she offers the following:

> Your responsibility as a parent is not so great as you might imagine. You need not supply the world with the next conqueror of disease or major

motion-picture star. If your child simply grows up to be someone who does not use the word "collectible" as a noun, you can consider yourself an unqualified success. [25]

and

Do not have your child's hair cut by a real hairdresser in a real hairdressing salon. He is, at this point, far too short to be exposed to contempt.[26]

and

If you are truly serious about preparing your child for the future, don't teach him to subtract—teach him to deduct.[27]

and

Ask your child what he wants for dinner only if he's buying.[28]

The last three examples contain generic *he,* but that does not make Lebowitz an antifeminist. Rather, she is a free spirit, whose causes are her own, a truly autonomous Self.

Lebowitz's one-liners are reminiscent of Bombeck's. The last quote reveals her solution to the challenge of cooking: Eat out. Lebowitz may be single, childless, and urban, but her attitude toward life is simply a more bohemian version of Erma. She too is struck with the unpleasantness of cleaning house. Her apartment was so dirty, she proclaimed, "Ashes to ashes, dust to dust." Her solution, however, was not to do the yucky job herself. "There was no question about it, I needed a maid, and needed one badly."[29] Since she didn't know how to go about recruiting one, Fran turned to a friend for help. "She regretted, however, that since I was looking for someone to come only one day a week, I could not expect the sort of high-quality service that was routinely available on her own premises." Lebowitz waited patiently until her friend phoned to say she had some candidates ready to be interviewed— "and by interview, she stressed *she did not mean asking them where they got their ideas or if they had always been funny,* but rather, where else they were employed, how much they charged and exactly what duties they were willing to perform."[30]

The foibles of everyday life are somewhat different in the two authors, but their approach is equally zany. Both supply instant energy. They give nutty advice with a straight face. They implicitly tell you not to take yourself or the world too seriously. "Housework, if you do it right, can kill you." (Bombeck) "If he didn't dust American furniture there was little chance he did windows." (Lebowitz) They are both watching their weight. (A permanent theme in Bombeck; for Lebowitz's advice, see "The Fran Lebowitz High Stress Diet and Exercise Progam.")

There is only so much you can do with wit as a tool, just as linguistic change is but a single weapon in the arsenal of women's liberation. Since humor and linguistic ability are mutually dependent, there would seem to be something worth pondering here. Friedan thought humor was out of place among feminists when contemplating domestic horrors like wax buildup, yet Bombeck's dictum "Guilt is the gift that keeps on giving" allows for both laughter *and* consciousness-raising. It is irreverent, the first quality necessary for shaking patriarchal institutions both at home and in the market place.

Notice the implications for change in Stephanie Brush's answer to the question, "Are men really superior in any way?"

> In some areas. For example, most men can throw a softball or a large rock farther than a woman can, and on that basis alone it's obvious men deserve to be president of AT & T.[31]

Brush is somewhere between Bombeck and Lebowitz. Though a single career woman, she explores the new domesticity of live-ins. To the question, "Why get married?" she replies: "Married people get better dishes and feel comfortable referring to knives and forks as 'flatware.' "[32] This sounds like Lebowitz, whose ignorance of Middle America is bliss. But to the question "Should men be allowed to 'bond'?" she sounds very much like Bombeck:

> Absolutely. It's important for grown men to get together with no women around and do close, intimate things like putting out lighted cigarettes on each other's arms, watching rigged sporting events on television and belching competitively. The other thing they do is to tell each other how bald they are, which a woman can never understand. No woman has ever looked a close friend in the eye and said, "My, you're looking quite the grizzled hag today, Betty."[33]

Bombeck reveals her impressions of men and children much in the same way that Brush discusses her live-ins. That is another ploy that antedates feminism—the reduction of the male to childishness. It may have arisen because of women's historic treatment at the hands of men—the "lady" must be construed as a helpless childish person (thus the use of "hon" and "dear" by strangers). It may also have originated in the female's stereotype as Earth Mother and Bearer of Culture, that is, the one who automatically takes charge of the *domesticum*. Both sexes should be accorded a degree of childishness or at least playfulness. Women with a sense of humor abound though men may not have noticed. A witty man is called "brilliant"; a witty woman is a shrew and a ballbreaker.

Humor, I believe, is essential to any program of social change. A too serious view of life has hampered both feminists and antifeminists in their recruitment of followers. Reverence for ideals led feminists to sign their letters "Yours in sisterhood," and reverence for patriarchal institutions led Phyllis Schlafly to defend motherhood and apple pie from the Equal Rights Amendment. One needs humor in order to prevent oneself from falling into fanaticism and becoming a bore. Even Bombeck's bored "martyress" is funny. "As with most heroines, there are few who are appreciated in their lifetime. One cannot possibly understand the awesome responsibility they shoulder." Therefore Bombeck nominated "overworked, underpatienced, unappreciated Lorraine Suggs . . . Mother Martyress." Her husband is out of town for a week, and if we had walked around in Suggs' wedgies, we would sympathize. For example,

> On Friday at the supermarket, so bored she was carrying on a conversation with a broom display, she went through the mechanics of shopping . . . lashing one kid to the basket, getting another out of the bean display where he "found" a hole in a bag of pinto beans, and on finding the third had eaten an unknown amount of fruit, offered to weigh him and anything over fifty-three pounds, pay the difference. The checkout girl in noting all the convenience foods said: "You're lucky to have your husband gone a lot. At least you don't have to cook big meals."[34]

This digression into humor has implications for titles and terms of endearment. Bombeck talks about housewives (invariably housewives who are also mothers like herself); Brush talks about single career women who have "live-ins" and therefore domestic chores to divide between them; Lebowitz is a single career woman who, so far as I can tell from *Social Studies* and the earlier *Metropolitan Life*, disdains "live-ins." She remains a real loner, which is perfectly understandable when you read about the housing situation in New York (see "The Pen of My Aunt Is on the Operating Table" and "Diary of a New York

Apartment Hunter." *Social Studies,* pp. 78–83 and 97–102). Therefore, she does not have a problem with a name for her current "boyfriend"; she mentions love affairs (at least two very complicated affairs—a recommendation to be found in "The Fran Lebowitz High Stress Diet and Exercise Program," *Social Studies,* pp. 125–130).

Thus, Erma refers to Mr. Bombeck as her "husband"; Fran is not troubled by word choice when it comes to her POSSLQ (Person of Opposite Sex Sharing Living Quarters), for she apparently resists having to live in the same apartment with anyone else. Stephanie prefers company at home, and that leaves her with the problem of how to describe him. She rejects "boyfriend," "my guy," "my old man," and "my lover" (and so would most of the rest of us, I suspect). That raises the question of why she herself can pass as someone's "girlfriend," but her "boyfriend" has no appropriate designation.

I suggest that the dilemma parallels the argument over "Ms."— resistance to accord females the same naming rights as males, that is, a title that does not disclose their marital status. Brush apparently uses the man's name only ("Al"), but her interviewer pressed for a *label.* "Al" should be sufficient at a party with strangers or even at a party in one's own home. If men and women shared equal social status, there would be no need to reveal their intimate living arrangements. Names should suffice, but people (not just men) often exhibit an insatiable curiosity about who's sleeping with whom. It's really none of their business.

Titles, names, and terms of endearment when used in a condescending manner can be irately rejected by the woman on whom they are thrust, but what if you're a housewife-mother from Queens, a lawyer, a former district attorney, a member of the House of Representatives, and your party's candidate for Vice President? You're wooing Democrats in the Deep South, where suspicion of Yankees and traditional attitudes toward women are entrenched. Such was Geraldine Ferraro's plight in 1984 when she was confronted by Jim Buck Ross, agriculture commissioner of the state of Mississippi. When she admitted that she hadn't yet sampled the catfish, Ross remarked, "Then you haven't lived, young lady." (Ferraro was 48; Ross, 70.)[35] Is this a polite title or a condescending one? "Young lady" is quite distinct from "lady," which is invariably sarcastic when used in the vocative case (that is, in direct address).

The author of the article makes no comment, and Ferraro was evidently too busy anticipating Ross's next question to give away via facial expression whether she was offended or even baffled. You have to be on your toes when you deal with Southerners; their good-old-boy exterior often disarms you. After commenting on the raising of blueberries, Ross pounced: "Can you make a blueberry muffin?"

The reporter speculates on the answers she might have given:

> Now what should have been Ms. Ferraro's response? Indignation? A sharp dismissal that such a question was inappropriate? The demand for a resolution by NOW attacking Jim Buck Ross for "insensitivity" and urging a boycott of Mississippi farm products?
>
> Ms. Ferraro did nothing of the kind. Instead, she smiled and replied, "Sure can." Then, after a beat, *she turned back to Jim Buck Ross and smiled,* "Can you?"[36]

Now it was Ross's turn to miss a beat! He replied that "in the South, men don't do the cooking, and about *how pretty Mississippi and New York women are.*" (Can you believe this?) The columnist, Jeff Greenfield, gave Ferraro high marks for this display of quick-witted but courteous table-turning.

> . . . the key political point is that Representative Ferraro gave clear and compelling evidence that she is going to be able to finesse the inevitable questions surrounding her candidacy. Based on this early exchange, she appears to understand that a measure of patience and a firm grip on her sense of humor will be the keys to her success as a candidate.[37]

Greenfield wrote that Ferraro had to be prepared to deal with questions and doubts "of the most irrational sort. . . . She may not like the fact that some voters want a woman to stay home with the children, but she is savvy enough to play to that sentiment, noting carefully that she chose to defer her career until the kids were grown."

Having lived in the South for a dozen years (the last two in the Deep South—Louisiana), I would wager that Ross's conversation was not a spontaneous expression of traditional male prejudices but a carefully orchestrated scenario calculated to fluster the Yankee "Ms." Southern politicians are inscrutable to Northerners; they have developed "playing dumb" into a fine art and are capable of "innocent" needling of strangers while maintaining the bland and courteous demeanor of a perfect gentleman. Ferraro no doubt anticipated some sort of domestic interrogation designed to ruffle her feathers, and she passed the test. It seems clear, however, that Ross was not prepared for a question about his own culinary skills. He may well know how to make blueberry muffins, but he couldn't admit it and spoil his image.

Southern men generally do not cook unless it's their job, but even old-timers who hunt know what to do with the kill, whereas their wives may not. If you don't believe it, consult the men's section of *River Road Recipes,* a fabulous cookbook compiled by the Junior League of Baton Rouge, La., and now available nationally. My copy is dated 1963 and contains a recipe for "Coon à la Delta." After you and your trusty coon hound have caught and killed the beast, you put it in the bathtub and skin it. This is men's work, to my way of thinking; I have never even eaten "Coon à la Delta," much less prepared it, but it might be a tasty dish, what with the hot sauce you baste it with. All the game recipes in the men's section are heavy on spices.

Greenfield concludes his approving essay on Ferraro's strategy as follows:

> when she is confronted by a man with assumptions of a very different world, who wants to know about Ms. Ferraro's skills in home economics rather than macroeconomics, she is clever enough to answer him with a smile and a polite flick of a rapier, rather than with a 20-pound club of indignation.[38]

Greenfield then quotes "that famous male chauvinist Henry Higgins in another context about another lady, 'I think she's got it.' "

As more women are chosen for high office, it will be interesting to see how they wield the feminine mystique in their favor where necessary. Lecturing men on their benighted attitudes will not win votes. That Ferraro resisted the impulse to rebuke her host means that we can look forward to a new era of linguistic juggling and bizarre conversations that may amaze and ultimately educate men to respect feminine voices.

Ferraro's nomination struck a responsive chord among feminists and nonfeminists alike. Here is one reaction, written by Trisha Flynn, a columnist for *The Denver Post,* who deserves syndication so that she can reach a wider audience.

> When Mondale chose Ferraro as his running mate, I happened to be in Washington visiting my sister—a woman who leans so far to the right I sometimes wonder how she manages to stand up. And yet, despite all our

differences, when we heard the news, we smiled. Both of us. At each other. Together. This particular sister of mine would probably slit her throat before she'd vote for a Democrat. Yet, for that moment, she smiled a thoroughly wonderful smile. She was able, however briefly, to identify perhaps for the first time, with her own sex.[39]

This temporary "bonding" by women across political barriers is a sign that the era of Simone de Beauvoir's "second sex" may be drawing to a close. "Ms." may not drive out "Miss" or "Mrs." in the near future, but let us hope that we do not have to abide the indignity of being "deared" and "honned" by total strangers. A strategy for letting our wishes be known with wit and tact would demonstrate both our intelligence and sense of humor. "Honning" and "dearing" back might alert the offender; a stronger response would be to address the instigator as "darling," thus escalating the phony intimacy.

7

The Language Gene

If I were to suggest that females possessed a language gene lacking in males, I would not be taken seriously, even though not too long ago a math gene surfaced in the press, a gene that was conveniently absent in females, for it explained boys' superiority in mathematics. Never mind that girls are socialized to believe that math is a male subject and that females are "naturally" poor at math. The "math anxiety" of women could be explained not as a culturally induced trauma but as a product of girls' defective genetic inheritance. Never mind that genes sort randomly or that a math gene had never been seen under a microscope. It was an idea whose time had come.

That is why I propose that women have a language gene: it explains why girls talk earlier than boys and handle language so well. It's a gift of Mother Nature and one that we should treasure, for most important ideas are conveyed by words, not numbers. Even mathematics can be translated into words, but the humanities and social sciences can scarcely be expressed in mathematical symbols. Thus, the female's language gene gives her the edge over males, who possess a *mere* math gene. If males had an early aptitude for language instead of for math, that's the way the case would be argued.[1]

Even admitting the chimerical nature of both math and language genes, I feel obliged to mention heredity, for no matter what topic a woman pursues, she is somewhere down the line attacked for being "unnatural." Nature vs. Nurture is at the heart of most debates about women's aspirations and capabilities. Granted, *homo sapiens* has an endowed capacity for language that is not found in other animals, but linguistic ability is unevenly spread among the population and cannot be proved to follow the lines of gender.

Josef E. Garai and Amram Scheinfeld published a monograph in 1968 asserting that girls indeed surpassed boys in verbal precocity: females began speaking sooner than males and from the age of eighteen months used more complex and sophisticated sentence patterns.[2] The authors attributed this linguistic achievement largely to socialization but admitted genetics into the argument to offer a possible explanation for boys' stuttering, poor articulation, aphasia, and dyslexia. Thus, most girls are verbally superior because of Nurture, whereas some boys are defective because of Nature—a sort of victory by default for the female.

Subsequent research efforts were far less supportive of the idea that females surpass males in early language acquisition and verbal fluency. Some empirical studies bore out Garai and Scheinfeld's conclusion, but many demonstrated that no superiority could be claimed for female children at all. For those that did maintain that girls developed linguistic fluency at a much earlier age than boys, the possibility that it was gene-linked was typically glossed over or not mentioned. Even Garai and Scheinfeld stressed environmental circumstances, such as intensive maternal interaction with daughters, to explain this area of female success. Their use of genetics was confined to explaining why some boys might have pathological problems.

In 1981 Gisela Klann-Delius made an enormous contribution to the subject with an article that surveyed more than 150 publications.[3] It was her contention that no empirical research could establish whether girls were earlier and more fluent speakers than boys and that the pursuit of such ends was wrong-headed. The question, she wrote, was not whether there is a "deficit" between the sexes, but whether there is a "difference." This change of emphasis characterizes feminist research in general, shifting the argument from "Who's better—girls or boys?" to "How do boys and girls differ?" This change of venue from the battle ground ("Who won the war?"), the playing field ("Who won the game?"), and the courtroom ("Who won the case?")—all masculine arenas—introduced a noncompetitive perspective on sex-related behaviors. "Differences" need not be assumed to be good or bad, guilty or innocent, but merely characteristic of one sex or the other, though on this point Klann-Delius reports that empiricism has so far failed to prove anything. Let us assume for a moment that the author is correct: If we cannot assert with any confidence that girls are more verbally proficient than boys, the issue of whether or not girls' superiority is genetic becomes moot.

However, male members of the linguistic Praetorian Guard have written about female users of English as if women have no right to demonstrate anything but the most utilitarian proficiency—enough to praise and serve their masters. When women have spoken or written eloquently, they have more often been damned than praised, and those who write about language itself are treated to the metaphorical punishment of promiscuous Vestal Virgins—buried in sand up to their necks until silenced. Whatever genetics may reveal about male vs. female innate linguistic ability, many men assume that they alone have inherited the right to control and regulate Mother Tongue. Women who invade this "serious" turf of intellectual discourse may well be branded as usurpers or revolutionaries.

Some women have great linguistic gifts, but when they speak, no matter how eloquently, they do not have the powerful impact of a man. The same is true of writing. Woman's writing has often been ascribed to a male; if her agency is admitted, then what she wrote is attacked on moral grounds; if morally acceptable, it is downgraded on esthetic grounds, i.e., it isn't art; its subject matter is domestic or regional or some other label that trivializes the work. If all else fails, the women's *oeuvre* is said to be scanty—one swallow does not make a summer; her work (artificially reduced in bulk by ignoring all but her best novel, say) is a fluke, virtually an accident. This is only a sample of the ingenious methods used by critics to keep women writers in their place—a limbo of literary losers. For details on this particularly invidious form of sexism, consult Joanna Russ's witty book *How to Suppress Women's Writing*.[4] If it weren't so sad, it would be funny. It is, in fact, appalling.

Russ counts the ways in which male critics have praised a genre used by a man and then blasted that same genre when used by a woman, for example, the confessional. The confessions of St. Augustine and Jean-Jacques Rousseau are works of genius; Kate Millett's *Flying* is mere confession. Russ accounts for some of the hostile or unfair criticism of women's writing as attributable to ignorance, habit, or sheer laziness, but certain bad reviews can be explained by the motive to protect male turf from encroaching invaders:

> the dim (or not-so-dim) perception that one's self-esteem or sex-based interests are at stake, the desire to stay within an all-male, all-white club that is, whatever its drawbacks, familiar and comfortable, and sometimes

the clear perception that letting outsiders into the club, economically or
otherwise, will disturb the structure of *quid pro quo* that keeps the club
going.[5]

The same motives can be found among critics who ridicule women
speakers or women who both speak and write in behalf of feminism.
No matter how gifted, how cogent, or how logical, a woman will be
criticized because she raises questions that disturb men's comfort,
their ease, their traditional status as Primary Being. Otherwise, it is
hard to account for Michael Levin's frenetic arguments against the title "Ms.," George F. Will's characterization of "libbers'" assault on linguistic sexism as "Stakhanovite witlessness," and other males' heated
objections to women's "tampering" or "meddling" with *our* (i.e., male)
language.

One of the most scathing keepers of English is John Simon, who defends Lady Language against the heathens in the full armor of God.
In his collection *Paradigms Lost* he devotes only one essay to women's
work on verbal sexism, but his injunctions are severe and caustic.[6] In
"Should We Genderspeak?" Simon reviews *Words and Women: New
Language in New Times* by Casey Miller and Kate Swift (1976), a book
that elicits his meanest and least convincing thoughts on language and
social reform.[7] The following passage captures some of his sarcasm
and contains a central fiat, denying women the right to make linguistic changes:

> Doubtless, women are entitled to the process of getting the rights and
> freedoms granted to men; once these goals are achieved, however, and
> even before that, they can leave language alone. When women have full
> social, political, and economic parity with men, no schoolgirl will burst
> into tears over *himself* being used in the sense of *herself* too, or about
> "men and women" being a more common phrase than "women and men"
> —any more than French schoolgirls, I imagine, weep over their sexual
> organs being, in both high and low parlance, of the masculine gender.[8]

There are implicit commands in this maddening summary of women
and language.[9] Language seems to belong to men; women should not
maul it, but if they must (or if we men can't prevent them), they
should cease and desist not only after they have achieved social, political, and economic parity with men but "even before that." It is not explained (1) why women should be shackled linguistically and (2) why

women should stop rearranging Mother Tongue *before* they have achieved parity with men.

It would seem that women do not have the same verbal rights as men when it comes to change and innovation. Why this should be so is not clear except that Simon, who is extremely proprietary about his adoptive tongue, is on guard against any and all attempts to "degrade" it. Feminists are only one object for his wrath and not the most worthy adversary. He seems to be playing tennis with the net down, saving his most delicious barbs for more challenging opponents.

As to why women should call a ceasefire on the linguistic front before the war is over, one might infer that he assumes the feminist panzer divisions, once rolling, will break though the Maginot Line (to borrow a metaphor from Michael Levin). There is a tacit admission that language may prove an ally in the war on sexism, that the war will be won, but even before the white flag goes aloft, militant women should lay down their arms and resume "normal" speech. Why should there be no permanent change in language to reflect women's new place in society?

Let us look once more at the passage quoted above, focusing now on the latter part:

> no schoolgirl will burst into tears over *himself* being used in the sense of herself too . . . any more than French schoolgirls, I imagine, weep over their sexual organs being, in both high and low parlance, of the masculine gender.

This sentence must be subjected to *explication de texte* in order to uncover the frail and biased nature of Simon's argument. First, the reference to weeping schoolgirls. This sexist stereotype is too shopworn to require comment. The prospect of students (male or female) weeping over any grammatical construction these days should gladden an English teacher's heart. If they felt strongly about our Mother Tongue, we might have less difficulty in restoring the literacy that Simon says has been lost. Schoolgirls in tears would alert Simon that something is wrong with generic *he* and with the fact that the word for female genitalia has masculine gender in French. Must female students *cry* before their perception of the inequality of the sexes is taken seriously? It seems a peculiar criterion at best and demonstrates Simon's pervasive condescension. Furthermore, generic *he* in English and masculine gender in French are not parallel constructions. The gender of nouns in Indo-European languages does not reflect sexism, or if it does (a dubious proposition), it is not on the agenda of reform by American feminists.

Simon admits that he has "never been a scholar of linguistics"; when asked to write a column on language in 1976, he believed that this lack of training "was actually an advantage."[10] He glories in amateur status, but he brands Miller and Swift as "women journalists"—obviously not in the same league with himself, a former teacher of English. In the introduction of *Paradigms Lost* he informs us that he was fluent in three languages at the age of four—Serbo-Croatian, Hungarian, and German.[11] This impressive evidence of linguistic precocity seems to give him the edge over Miller and Swift, who claim no knowledge of foreign languages. A linguist would agree that Simon is not a linguist: he is a polyglot. Linguists would accord both Simon and the authors of *Words and Women* amateur status. However, Simon went on to acquire both French and English, giving him a five-to-one advantage over Miller and Swift.[12] Yet the number of languages studied and even mastered does not make one a linguist. He remains an amateur. To be sure, as an English teacher Simon can claim more technical knowledge of grammar and usage than those who have never taught English. I do not deny that he has an astonishing grasp of his adoptive language or argue that he should be dismissed because English is not his mother tongue. What I object to is his proprietary attitude, his self-appointed position as arbiter and protector of the language. With such a lofty view of himself, his cheap shot at Miller and Swift as sexually ambiguous is indefensible.

> I am deeply worried when the authors define *androgyny* . . . as "that rare and happy wholeness," a state that, *judging from their jacket photographs, they may indeed have achieved.* In no sense, figurative or literal, do I take hermaphroditism to be a happy state of affairs.[13]

My italics mark a dangling participle, an error that Simon should be ashamed of. *Judging* modifies *they* (Miller and Swift), whereas Simon, the viewer of the jacket photograph, is the one doing the judging.

Simon is against singular *they*, as in "Every*one* picked up their coat." He contends that although this construction may indeed be found in the best writers (as Miller and Swift contend), such lapses are just that —lapses, errors, slips of the pen. "Some*one* cannot be they."[14] Some*one* cannot be *he* either for the stylist who demands agreement in both gender and number. Simon does not consider lack of agreement in gender worthy of discussion.

At the end of his review he provides us an insight to the World According to Simon, where language must preserve order on Planet Earth.

> I doubt whether women's visibility will be achieved by calling usherettes ushers, or replacing *mankind* with the Miller-Swift coinage *genkind.* Equal job opportunities, salaries, and recognition are what will make women fully visible, something to be achieved *not by meddling with language but by political action.*[15]

Like Lakoff, Simon asserts that political change must precede linguistic change; also like Lakoff, Simon takes a dim view of women's slap-happy neologisms. Lakoff, however, recommended that innovators submit their new words to a board of linguists, who would pass judgment on the etymology and suitability of neologisms before they were allowed to enter the lexicon. Simon would not qualify for Lakoff's board of inquiry since he is proudly a nonlinguist.

Men who criticize women for linguistic innovation frequently use the verb "meddle" or "tamper." Meddling and tampering imply lack of authorization, lack of proper training, lack of justifiable motive. If women "meddle" with language, the language is bound to suffer. It is one thing for women to speak out against injustice; it is quite another for them to presume to alter Mother Tongue! Men like Simon make it apparent that Mary Daly's claim that women have had the power of naming stolen from them is not far from the truth. I used to think Daly's dictum was hyperbolic; now I consider it only slightly flawed: women never had the power of naming in the first place.

Simon's last paragraph in his attack upon Miller and Swift echoes Michael Levin, who felt that the title "Ms." might slow down the reproduction of the species:

> Yet woe betide if this is accomplished at the cost of sacrificing womanliness in women and manliness in men. Men and women must continue to attract each other through characteristics peculiar to their respective sexualities and sexes; a world in which we cease to be sexually fascinating to one another through certain differences will be a world well lost. And this may be a very real danger to—not mankind, not womankind, and certainly not genkind. To humankind.[16]

This peroration does not prompt me to grab for my hankie. It is not a moving piece of prose: it is bathos. Are we to believe that abolition of generic *he* and the suppresion of such insulting gender-marked words as "Jewess" and "Negress" will deprive the sexes of their intrinsic "fascination" for each other?[17] Apparently so. Feminists' "tampering" with the language will disguise the anatomical and hormonal structure of the sexes to the extent that the world won't be fit to live in. Suicide seems to be the only solution when female language-manglers are finished. A grim prospect indeed.

The implicit imperative in this cosmic discourse orders women to stop meddling with the language in the name of equality before their destructive and misguided fanatacism brings reproduction—or at least romance—to a grinding halt. Experts in population control, take note: your troubles are over. Worldwide hunger can be eradicated in our lifetime through the simple expedient of letting "Women's Libbers" loose on the language.

The imperative mood governs the language of myth, as Elizabeth Janeway pointed out in *Man's World, Woman's Place,* and myth is substituted for rational discourse whenever conservatives wish to keep women in their "place."[18] She fingered Phyllis McGinley who wrote that women and men should stay in their own spheres (home and marketplace, respectively). McGinley does not claim that women will be better off, but *society* will. Women, the "sacrificers" and "self-immolators," have the responsibility of keeping the planet in orbit.[19] A language-meddler by virtue of being a poet, McGinley is never attacked by the male establishment since she shares their most profound beliefs. Her poetry does not threaten the patriarchal family. Consequently, she may tamper with words to her heart's content. Only those women who challenge sexist assumptions are at risk: they have no right to alter Mother Tongue, and though they are trivialized and ridiculed, these "libbers" are viewed as threats not only to decent English but to the social order as well. In short, men claim the right to control *our* Mother Tongue.

In *Language and Woman's Place,* Robin Lakoff jumped on a bizarre genetic bandwagon—the one belonging to Lionel Tiger, anthropologist at Rutgers. Lakoff found that Tiger's male "bonding" theory offered a plausible explanation for notable differences between men's and women's behavior. Lakoff summarizes the thesis of Tiger's book *Men in Groups:* men "hunted together in packs, while the women stayed behind, caring for their individual living sites and raising the children."[20] Men had to work together, in order to complete the job successfully. " . . . basically the males directed their efforts toward a

common goal; among the females, each had her own goal and succeeded as an individual."[21] This ancient training in cooperation—
male bonding—can be seen in current male control of all major institutions.

Lakoff accepts Tiger's explanation for male supremacy but di-
verges from his pessimistic belief that such an old pattern cannot be
broken. She believes that people have demonstrated a capacity to
change over time, that men might be encouraged to bond less;
women, more. In fact, Lakoff sees a tendency among women toward
bonding,

> a sense of female camaraderie, though it is still a camaraderie of the un-
> derdog. . . . But perhaps even more important, for women and for the
> human race generally, is establishing patterns of bonding between both
> sexes, so that women, with their special abilities, sensitivities, and talents
> may be integrated into the "real world"; and men, with theirs, may learn
> to function more smoothly in the home.[22]

Lakoff refers to Tiger in the context of Part II of her book, "Why
Women Are Ladies," and ladies' education discourages bonding. Ladylike behavior includes deference, distance, and superpolite usage.
"Women's language avoids the markers of camaraderie: backslapping, joke telling, nicknaming, slang, and so forth."[23] Women in
groups substitute embracing for backslapping, personal remarks for
jokes. In mixed company women drop *all* signs of camaraderie, but
even in all-women groups female camaraderie is not as marked as that
of men. Lakoff finds utility in male bonding:

> men can tell dirty jokes and slap each other's backs even when they can't
> stand each other; this is presumably how a great deal of the world's work
> gets done. But women embrace and share confidences only when there
> are real feelings of sympathy betwen them.[24]

This seems to be an argument for developing both a thick skin and a
phony friendliness on the part of women, since bonding is being promoted as a tool wherewith to get the world's work done. This advice
would turn off feminists who resist suggestions that women should
adopt any type of male behavior simply because men are in control of
our institutions, and this includes language, which I will return to
shortly. It is Tiger's "bonding" theory that I wish to pursue for the
moment.

In "Male Dominance? Yes, Alas. A Sexist Plot? No." Tiger shows "concern" for feminists, who have adopted the outdated premises of Pavlovian biology.[25] In an attempt to instruct Kate Millett (his *bête noire*) he points out the need to recognize real (as opposed to cultural) differences between the sexes. Dr. Katharina Dalton's work on PMS is stressed (many women being incapacitated before, during, and after menstruation, not to mention menarche and menopause—equally hysterical times in the life of the female). Though he denies that hormonal imbalance should be used as evidence that women are unfit for high-level jobs, the overall impression of his article is that anatomy is still destiny. For example (on keeping Mom at home): "the fact that the whole human species has overwhelmingly elected to have children raised at least in the first years by women suggests conformity to nature rather than to male conspiracy." Leaving male conspiracy aside as a straw man and an artificial choice, I wonder if Tiger believes that whatever people have done over the long haul is "natural" and should therefore continue to be done. If so, the women's movement is worthless by definition. Once again we are warned in the mythic imperative mood to follow nature, or else.

> Our biological heritage is the product of millions of years of successful adaptation and it recurs in each generation with only tiny alterations. It is simply prudent that those concerned with changing sex roles understand the possible biological importance of what they want to do, and take careful measure of what these phenomena mean. If they do not, the primary victims of their misanalysis, unfortunately, will be—as usual—women and their daughters.[26]

Throughout the article but especially here Tiger's emphasis on the millions of years behind *homo sapiens* (coupled with his belief that behavior enters our DNA but very slowly) can be construed as a threat, a charge of deserved guilt if we don't heed the message of Science and Nature. Since it takes millions of years for a new behavior to become fixed in our genetic structure, we must be prepared to *wait*.

WASPs generally sympathize in retrospect with civil rights demands by blacks, who were asked to be patient 100 years after the Emancipation Proclamation; they are not nearly so sympathetic with women. Tiger, arguing from statistics and the weight of tradition, says Nature explains the fact that most children are cared for by females. He might just as well have argued that statistically and traditionally women have been subordinate to males and therefore should remain so. If you read between the lines, that in fact is his message in a nutshell.

A refutation of sexist anthropologists can be found in an article by Sally Slocum—"Woman the Gatherer: Male Bias in Anthropology."[27] There are several lines of argument here, but the most damaging evidence against Tiger et al. is this:

> Every human individual gets half its genes from a male and half from a female; *genes sort randomly. It is possible for a female to end up with all her genes from male ancestors, and for a male to end up with all his genes from female ancestors.* The logic of the hunting argument would have us believe that all the selection pressure was on the males, leaving the females simply as drags on the species. The rapid increase in brain size and complexity was thus due entirely to half the species; the main function of the female half was to suffer and die in the attempt to give birth to their large-brained male infants. An unbiased reading of the evidence indicates there was selection pressure on both sexes, and that hunting was not in fact the basic adaptation of the species from which flowed all the traits we think of as specifically human. Hunting does not deserve the primary place it has been given in the reconstruction of human evolution . . . .[28]

If genes sort randomly, then women are as likely to possess hunting-bonding genes as men are, and men have a share of gathering non-bonding genes. Moreover, Slocum argues that women in primitive society needed cooperative and communicative skills in order to gather sufficient food for the group. The vegetation that they collected along with the small game they caught accounted for 8o percent of the food supply needed for survival, a figure that Tiger does not contest. In fact, the highly touted big hunts of the men provided a treat, a feast, but not the staple of ancient diets by any stretch of the imagination.

Slocum contends that the first "man-made" items of primitive society were a sling for the baby and a sack for gathering plants; she further challenges the identification of the earliest surviving artifact as a weapon; rather, she thinks it might just as well have been a tool for scraping animal hides. She asks, Why would women be totally isolated at "home" when it would make more sense to assume that women worked together and therefore developed cooperative communicative skills in gathering food (which included hunting small game) and taking care of the children? Since women are generally sociable creatures today, there is no reason to depict them as isolated, antisocial, and uncooperative in the distant past.

Tiger adduces sports, fraternities, and the American Legion as evidence of ancient male bonding. Women during the era of the feminine mystique were urged to acquire status by moving to the suburbs in discrete dwellings with appliances that made tract houses maximally self-sufficient, yet as we know from Betty Friedan, if not from our own experience, women so isolated suffered psychic anguish. Shopping trips in the obligatory station wagon, P.T.A. meetings, cub scouts and Little League did not fill the social gap. Only at the beauty parlor, bridge parties, and Kaffeeklatsches did women socialize for their own enjoyment rather than for the benefit of the family, and it was at a Kaffeeklatsch in 1959 that Friedan first heard about "the problem that has no name." Women on farms who cleaned, cooked, and shared the duties of child raising among female relatives seem to have fared better. They also had quilting bees where they could create a work of art and swap stories at the same time. Since Tiger and others have freely drawn upon modern institutions to reconstruct their picture of primitive society, I see no reason to limit myself in this regard. The quilting bee, to my mind, is as relevant to primitive woman as the American Legion is to primitive man. You may take neither or both as you wish, but to accept only the male "bonding" thesis, flimsy a construction as it is, would not seem quite fair.

Tiger very nearly says that erect bipedalism and language grew out of the men's big hunt, a theory that leaves women crawling around on all fours saying "Ugh ugh." How does he explain the female's precocity in language development, a fact acknowledged even by Freud? We have heard a great deal about boys' superiority in math and spatial relations, while girls' early speaking ability is glossed over as somehow less important. In some cases its genetic base is denied, and early female linguistic development is attributed to intensive maternal interaction with daughters. If female infants' remarkable demonstration in speaking early can be explained as culturally determined, then boys' math gene should be dismissed as counterfeit, for we know that males are encouraged in math while girls are discouraged (or have been until the past few years).

Lakoff's use of Tiger seems anomalous, but she recommended his "bonding" as a trait that could be learned by women. If Tiger insists that bonding is in the DNA, then she was wrong to take so optimistic a view. I believe (with Lakoff) that bonding is possible for women. An outstanding proof is Phyllis Schlafly's "Eagle Forum," a large group of women attracted by Schlafly's message as well as her demonstrable charisma to spend hours campaigning against the Equal Rights Amendment without the inducement of money. These women, for the most part housewives, were motivated by love of family and country to flock to state capitals all over the United States, bringing home-made apple pie to eager legislators. If these gingham-clad mothers had been recruited early on by feminist organizations, we might now have an E.R.A. instead of a polarized female population. Perhaps the sociobiologists with their more sophisticated variation on the theme "Anatomy is destiny" will find that women have an apple pie gene. I think it more likely that they will work on the sinister implications of Pre-Menstrual Syndrome to delay women's accession to full citizenship. Feminists, I think, have learned their lesson the hard way: women can learn to bond in no time, and Schlafly's ability to mobilize them proves that they can bond for any cause if properly wooed. Now that feminists are belatedly mending fences, slurs against housewife-mothers are scarcely heard. We may expect an olive branch of linguistic buzz words to emerge that will praise women—*all* women, not just those who are doggedly following men up the corporate ladder in three-piece suits. A straw in the wind is Geraldine Ferraro's statement that she (like Edith Bunker) is a housewife from Queens.

Whether female linguistic ability turns out to be gene-linked or not, women are continually reminded of their mysterious connection with Nature (Jung's "Eternal Feminine") in a way that men are not. In fact, Mother Nature has been used to thwart women's ambitions to such an extent that the subject of heredity goes down poorly in feminist circles. Should women possess greater innate capacity for speech, feminists would be loath to accept this advantage over males, for it would be turned into a disadvantage by antifeminists. This is why they view with shock the plea of Pre-Menstrual Syndrome as the basis of an acquittal in a murder trial: it revives the image of women as weak, sick, and unstable.

The jury is not yet in on the debate over girls' demonstration of linguistic precocity, but whether it is attributable to Nature, Nurture, or a combination, the way that women perceive the world is different from that of men. The implications of women's utterances, both verbal and written, are immense, as has been pointed out by Sally McConnell-Ginet, Ruth Borker, and Nelly Furman.

> Scholarship on women's relation to language has by no means been confined to consideration of the views and linguistic practices of women who identify themselves as feminists. Careful analysis of what women say (and write) and how they say it is proving a very powerful tool for gaining insight into women's lives. Coupled with attention to what others say to and of women and how it is said, such investigations show that *women's experience is not always expressed in the ways that male-centered analyses might lead us to expect.*[29]

One such piece of male-centered analysis is William M. O'Barr and Bowman K. Atkins' "'Women's Language' or 'Powerless Language'"?[30] The authors apparently attribute the perceived weakness of women's language to cultural factors rather than to inheritance. So far, so good. However, their suggestion to change the term "women's language" to "powerless language" strikes me as a handy way to dilute the issue, to make "women's language" disappear as a concept by renaming it. In short, "women's language" would become a subset of "powerless language" if O'Barr and Atkins had their way, and such a subordination of women's behavior was the norm in scholarship until the 1970s. Females have either been ignored altogether or mentioned in passing as if they constituted a fringe element or a negligible entity. O'Barr and Atkins do not appear to be biased against women, yet the conclusion of their article goes against the grain of recent feminist research. One senses that the authors are uncomfortable with the term "women's language" and therefore wish to abolish it.

To make such an assertion about so compelling a piece of research, I am obliged to present a synopsis of their findings. Their article focuses on women as witnesses in a courtroom setting. O'Barr, professor of anthropology at Duke University, was director of the Law and Language Project at Duke (1974–77), from which this special investigation emerged. The authors give credit to Lakoff's *Language and Woman's Place:* " . . . her work was for us—as it was for many others— a jumping off point."[31] In fact, they use her criteria for evaluating the speech of female witnesses, but first—and this makes their study unique in my experience—they provide a brief description of what handbooks for lawyers say about how to treat women in court. One of the trial practice manuals from which they quote was co-authored by F. Lee Bailey and includes the following advice:

> Women are contrary witnesses. They hate to say yes. . . . A woman's desire to avoid the obvious answer will lead her into your real objective—contradicting the testimony of previous prosecution witnesses. *Women, like children, are prone to exaggeration; they generally have poor memories as to previous fabrications and exaggerations.* They also are stubborn. You will have difficulty trying to induce them to qualify their testimony. Rather, it might be easier to induce them to exaggerate and cause their testimony to appear incredible. *An intelligent woman will very often be evasive.* She will avoid making a direct answer to a damaging question. *Keep after her until you get a direct answer—but always be the gentlemen.*"[32]

That such advice could have been published by eminent attorneys as late as 1971 says much about our society—especially the comparison of women with children, the need to specify that some women have brains and will avoid blurting out something stupid, and the assumption that all lawyers are men. Another major point made in the trial practice manuals is to avoid provoking the female witness to tears, for a crying woman may sway the jurors away from sympathy with you, the lawyer.

O'Barr and Atkins then offer samples and evaluations of the speech of female witnesses in the Durham County (North Carolina) Superior Court, using Lakoff's book as a guide to "women's language."* They find that not all women use "women's language" but that some men do, although in no case did a man employ the intonational features of women.[33] Women professionals who routinely appear in court (e.g., a pathologist) did not exhibit what the authors abbreviate to WL, whereas a housewife appearing in court for the first time exhibited virtually all of Lakoff's WL features. Similarly, men of low socio-economic status unaccustomed to giving testimony at a trial scored

*There is a mistake here, for they say "she provides no firm listing of the major features of what she terms 'women's language' . . . ," and so they drew up their own list of features. Lakoff lists nine features *(LAWP,* pp. 53–56); O'Barr and Atkins list ten ("'Powerless Language?'" p. 96). They separate tag questions from question intonation where declarative intonation is expected (Nos. 3 and 10); Lakoff combines them in her No. 3. They include *so* under "speaking in italics" and call it "emphatic" (their No. 4), whereas Lakoff calls *so* an "intensive" that is actually less emphatic than "very"; she puts *so* right after "hedges" (her No. 4) and says it is related to them; "speaking in italics"is her No. 9. Finally, O'Barr and Atkins (in their No. 8) have the following: *"Direct quotations* (use of direct quotations instead of paraphrases)," which is not a feature listed by Lakoff.

higher on WL features than the ambulance drivers who were both "professional" and familiar with court procedure. There were examples in between the ends of the spectrum for both men and women.

Although O'Barr and Atkins admit that WL characterized the speech of female witnesses more than of males, they state:

> Taken together these findings suggest the so-called "women's language" is neither characteristic of all women nor limited only to women. A similar continuum of WL features (high to low) is found among speakers of both sexes. These findings suggest that the sex of a speaker is insufficient to explain incidence of WL features, and that we must look elsewhere for an explanation of this variation.[34]

After rating witness transcripts as to high or low in WL features, they subjected their data to an interesting test: they took the high WL speech and had actors and actresses speak the lines onto tape; then they edited out the WL features, modifying the WL speech so that it was straightforward and devoid of hedges and hesitations (the edited versions were also taped by actors and actresses). The "powerful" and "powerless" (or WL) versions were each read by a male and a female (a total of four versions) and tested on a group of 96 undergraduates at the University of North Carolina in Chapel Hill.[35] It should come as no surprise that the "powerful" versions elicited more favorable reactions from the students than did the "powerless" ones.[36] Yet the authors, wishing to rule out voice intonation as a variable, followed up this experiment with a written transcript representing "powerful" and "powerless" language, and came out with similar results.

As a conclusion to their article the authors suggest renaming "women's language" "powerless language," for in their opinion a high incidence of WL features is not sex-linked but is based on socio-economic status and prior experience in court. Their suggestion includes a criticism of Lakoff, whose "concept of 'women's language' is in need of modification."

> Lakoff's discussion of "women's language" confounds at least two different patterns of variation. Although our title suggests a dichotomy between "women's language" and "powerless language," these two patterns undoubtedly interact. It could well be that to speak like the powerless is not only typical of women because of the all-too-frequent powerless social position of many American women, but is also a part of the cultural meaning of speaking "like a woman."[37]

My major objection to this proposal and its rationale is that the term "powerless language" is not as accurate as "women's language" as described by Lakoff with the nuances, explanations, and examples laid out in her book. The word "powerless" conveys a totally negative impression, whereas Lakoff's feature No. 7—"Superpolite forms"—includes the qualification: "more positively, women are the repositories of tact and know the right things to say to other people. . . . "[38] This positive interpretation of "superpolite forms" is not mentioned by O'Barr and Atkins, but this aspect of Lakoff's concept together with other possibly good features of "women's language" are worth studying on their merits before they are discarded as merely "powerless."

Lakoff herself said that many if not all of her features do not necessarily characterize the speech of the majority of women; age and socio-economic status played a part. Men, too, could be found using features of what she termed "women's language." As I said earlier, she laid the goundwork for virtually all other studies on the subject— whether pro or con—in the decade following publication of her book in 1975. Since women—even by O'Barr's and Atkins' admission—use this type of speech more than men do, I think the term "women's language" should and will be retained. Besides, their sample was limited to the testimony of witnesses in Durham County Superior Court, a setting that represents a highly limited sample of the way women speak.

Furthermore, O'Barr and Atkins assume that housewives have low status, with very little qualification.[39] That generalization in this particular study may be true, given the limited sample they present verbatim in their article, but it is not a truth: it is a truism, one that Erma Bombeck and countless others have disproven. The assertiveness of a housewife may be greater than that of a female professional. This represents the truth not only in the eighties but for some time in the past. I believe this not just with respect to Boulder County, Colorado, but also with respect to Durham County and also Orange County, North Carolina (the latter being the county of Chapel Hill), since I lived there from 1950 to 1961—the height of the "feminine mystique" when "women's language" was more in vogue than in 1974–77 when O'Barr and Atkins collected their court data.

It strikes me as peculiarly masculist that these authors would set up the dichotomy "powerful/powerless" in their "modification" of Lakoff, and I doubt that this particular form of reductionism will advance the study of the subject matter. Their suggested relabeling would appear to emanate from an androcentric value system that deserves scrutiny because of its unstated assumptions. O'Barr and Atkins, though fair and impartial, demonstrate by their unwarranted call for a relabeling of "women's language" the traditional neutralization of a feminist issue in the hands of even well-intentioned men. It is an illustration of what McConnell-Ginet, Borker, and Furman have said (quoted above): "women's experience is not always expressed in the ways that male-centered analyses might lead us to expect."

Admittedly, O'Barr and Atkins deserve praise for paying attention to what women witnesses said on the stand in North Carolina, for recognizing that "women's language" was an issue worth studying, and for using Lakoff to orient themselves in a "foreign" land. If they had merely corroborated (or *not* corroborated) Lakoff's description of "women's language," I would have no quarrel with them, but to equate her "women's language" with "powerless language" in general demonstrates a misreading of *Language and Woman's Place.* Moreover, their scrambling of Lakoff's nine categories into ten of their own because she purportedly had not provided a list shows a cavalier attitude toward the source from which they say they derived their inspiration.

I do not attribute this misunderstanding on their part to their genes but to their lack of zeal in pursuing a spin-off of their *real* research—the "Law and Language Project." The unfortunate impression on the reader is that Lakoff's book was not taken seriously by the authors who cite it. Hence, it is difficult to trust their editing of "women's language" utterances into "powerful language"; they provide no examples of their redactions. Since they have erroneously supplied a tenth trait that does not appear in Lakoff's list—"direct quotations"—I assume that this spurious datum was used in their rewrites and that their results are necessarily suspect.

O'Barr incorporated this research into his book *Linguistic Evidence: Language, Power, and Strategy in the Courtroom* (New York: Academic Press/Harcourt Brace Jovanovich, 1982). *Language and Woman's Place* is cited as "a catalyst and encouragement for many other researchers with rudimentary interests in the way women and men speak differently."[40] O'Barr had still not studied Lakoff's book with sufficient care to correct his earlier misconstruction:

What Lakoff proposed was that women's speech varies from men's in several significant ways. *Although she provided no firm listing of the major features of what she terms WOMEN'S LANGUAGE* . . . the following were said to occur in high frequency among women. This set of characteristics provided a baseline for investigating gender-related speech patterns in court.[41]

Number (8) of the ten supplied by O'Barr is "DIRECT QUOTA-TIONS: Use of direct quotations rather than paraphrases."[42] This trait is used in Table 5.1, "Frequency Distribution of Women's Language Features in the Speech of Six Witnesses," but the footnote informs us that direct quotations are not ordinarily allowed in court because of the rule against hearsay evidence.[43] Therefore, the occurrence of this feature was practically nil. Nevertheless, its appearance in O'Barr's work and his assertion once again that Lakoff did not include a "firm list" in her book casts a shadow of doubt over the conclusions he draws and his repeated equation of "women's language" with "powerless language." I can see why "Powerful versus Powerless Speech" would make sense as a subtitle in a chapter called "Speech Styles in the Courtroom," since lawsuits are either won or lost. As for the merging of "women's language" into "powerless language," I would prefer the Scottish legal option of "not proven."

8

Futurespeak

If "women's language" represents "oldspeak," it should be time to talk of "futurespeak," but I believe that the underlying forces that supported "women's language" are still very much with us. It is therefore appropriate to return to Lakoff, in particular to the second part of her book, "Why Women Are Ladies." Lakoff wrote that when presenting her ideas, she met with audience resistance: she was perceived as being anti-woman by both men and women critics.[1] The "separate-but-equal" status of women did not strike her hearers as anything but beneficent. This notion, in her opinion, revolves around the issue of "politeness," a concept drummed into us from childhood.

> . . . women's speech differs from men's in that women are more polite, which is precisely as it should be, since women are the preservers of morality and civility; and we speak around women in an especially "polite" way in return, eschewing the coarseness of ruffianly men's language: no slang, no swear words, no off-color remarks. Further, many of the ways we choose to speak of women reflect our higher estimate of them than of men, and exalt and flatter, rather than humiliate. So, the argument runs, my position, that women should be aware of these discrepancies in language and do what they can to demolish them, is the one that denigrates and degrades women.[2]

Lakoff examines this criticism by discussing "forms of politeness," admitting that both women's and men's styles of speech have their virtues, and then digging beneath the surface of the "politeness" veneer. In reality, men have power; women don't:

men make up the stereotypes, and groups typically don't invent stereotypes about themselves, but about other groups. Hence it is the dominant group in a society that establishes stereotypes of the other groups, and decides which groups, on the basis of these stereotypes, are "good" and "bad."[3]

Women, she says, have developed two ways of handling their own stereotyping by men, the powerful group: either by proving themselves aggressive or by sticking to their nonaggressive posture as a virtue. She declares the second position "a strong one," one that resists brainwashing by the powerful.[4]

Since women are less powerful than men, they are at men's mercy linguistically: men use endearments on women that they don't use on each other; men tell jokes at women's expense and are impervious to women's jokes (if any) in rebuttal; men exhibit camaraderie among themselves that they don't extend to women. "Men, in effect, say 'Stay away: our friendship doesn't include you.' "[5] Just as minority groups can tell jokes about other groups, men tell jokes about women. However, ethnic jokes (says Lakoff) are now (1975) considered offensive: ethnic minorities are perceived as part of the "anybody" that one cannot risk offending. The only group that does not constitute part of this newly perceived "anybody" is the female majority.[6]

Lakoff's analysis here can be seen as a variation of Simone de Beauvoir's thesis that men perceive men as "Self," women as "Other"; Beauvoir also pointed out that women were the only subordinate caste or class perennially referring to themselves as "they" instead of "we." Lakoff concludes her remarks, pitting "politeness" against "power," as follows:

> I have given reason to believe that the kinds of "politeness" used by and of and to women do not arise by accident; that they are, indeed, stifling, exclusive, and oppressive. But I don't feel that we must maintain the kinds of social relationships we have always assumed. If we are aware of what we're doing, why we're doing it, and the effects our actions have on ourselves and everyone else, we will have the power to change.[7]

And lest anyone charge her with labeling "women's language" as less valuable than men's, or women as less valuable human beings than men, here is the last sentence of *Language and Woman's Place*, a kind of envoi to her readers: "I hope this book will be one small first step in the direction of a wider option of life styles, for men and women."[8]

I consider it, on the contrary, a giant leap for womankind, full of good counsel and diplomatic insights, but firmly grounded in the realities of social, political and economic necessity. Lakoff offered some well-meant advice to an audience that in many cases was not yet ready to receive it. She resisted preaching to the converted—always an easier task—and yet even among feminists, who should have welcomed her with open arms, she met with criticism. Still, she managed to touch the feelings of both "ladies" and "feminists," so that they focused on language as an important aspect of their respectively conservative and liberal philosophies.

That some women would rather be accorded token courtesies than real respect was evident nine or ten years ago when Lakoff lectured about her book, answering questions from perplexed and sometimes hostile groups. I witnessed one such confrontation in Denver with Professor Lakoff ably fielding questions from all directions. Yet no matter how agile, she could not convince those who preferred "pedestal status." That this attitude has survived into the eighties is demonstrated by the following letter to *The Denver Post* from a local resident:

> For years I've done my share of muttering about the so-called women's lib movement. Thinking and muttering that most of these gals have never been treated like a lady or they would never be shouting about being equal. During most of my mutterings about these women wanting to be equal, I've always said I personally enjoyed being treated as superior. Thank you, gentlemen.
>
> My mother always told me to remember my pleases and thank yous. I'm still trying to figure out the logic behind the nomination of Geraldine Ferraro for Vice President. From what I've read about her, she's not too sure what she believes in. The only distinction I can see about her from the majority of other politicians, is the fact that she is a woman. She has a fair amount of intelligence which leaves me just a wee bit cold, because I always understood that wisdom came before intelligence.
>
> So, if we're looking for the best woman for the job, I cast my vote for Erma Bombeck—don't laugh, think about it.[9]

This letter reveals the sort of criticism that Lakoff alludes to in her book: the fear that assertiveness means leaving the pedestal; the assumption that women are superior to men and are treated as such (no mention of the wage differential, you'll notice); the false choice between courtesy and citizenship (as if one must quit saying "please" and "thank you" when one becomes politically active); the idea that "wisdom" must precede "intelligence" (intelligence is necessary for wisdom. Perhaps she means "common sense."); and finally the astonishing suggestion to run Erma Bombeck for national office. On this score, I have to admit that Bombeck is perhaps the most politically unifying woman in America. Neither her formidable intelligence nor her strong support for the E.R.A. apparently fazed the lady from Littleton. I expected the letter to end with a plug for Phyllis Schlafly. It would be comforting to think that the content of this letter represented only a small minority of American women but unlikely. The writer's endorsement of Bombeck is heartening, but the other views expressed are thoroughly unreconstructed.

A major issue for women of the eighties is whether they can succeed in traditionally male professions without adopting an exclusively masculine point of view. Feminists insist that women develop their own style and their own standards if they are to improve the work place rather than be transformed into female counterparts of the driven, power-mad, ulcerated characters represented by the worst male stereotypes. And now that home and hearth have been reestablished as worthy of the highest consideration, can women finally convince men that they have valuable insights to contribute both at home and at work? Women are not put down so easily by male condescension as they used to be. Even women who shun the label "feminist" are speaking up fearlessly on feminist issues. Men who were proud to be chauvinists have been known to man the barricades for a daughter denied access to a school sporting event or program. These same men are seldom willing to consider their wives' complaints about inequity. The proud father can still view his wife as a nag, unfortunately, no matter how carefully and unemotionally she chooses her words.

Words alone will not bring about the millennium, but they are useful in putting forward our cause. Gloria Steinem has some useful ideas on the utility of language. Assertiveness training, she claims, should be undertaken with caution if it teaches women merely how to parrot men. Women, who with their "intuition" are excellent listeners, should teach men this skill, for talking without listening is not a conversation. She offers "practical exercises for achieving a change in the balance of talk."[10] She goes so far as to suggest tape-recording a dinner-table conversation and passing out poker chips to participants who must give up a chip each time he or she talks. Steinem assumes that both men and women may be interrupters and that both men and women may be excessively quiet, but the premise of her article (borne out by linguistic investigations) is that men tend to domineer and interrupt conversation. Yet she does not assume that this is a gift of Nature or a result of past hunting experience. Rather, it is a behavior that can be changed. "Discussing the results of studies on who talks more can produce some *very healthy self-consciousness in both men and women.*"[11]

Michael Levin should attend one of these soirées and discover that his horror of self-conscious speech acts is unwarranted. Steinem stresses listening as a positive act, a trait not mentioned by Lakoff, though in *Language and Woman's Place* she called women "the repositories of tact," which might have covered the ability to listen attentively. Steinem agrees with Lakoff's description of "ladylike" as a double bind that is demanded of girls and then used against them when as adults they don't come across as forceful or serious. She adds, "Even Lakoff seems to assume, however, that female speech is to be criticized as the deficient form, while male speech is the norm and thus escapes equal comment."[12]

Steinem's "practical exercises" offer the following insights that suggest more work is needed on the linguistic front.

> Check the talk politics concealed in your own behavior. Does your anxiety level go up (and your hostess instincts quiver) when women are talking and men are listening, but not the reverse? For instance, men often seem to feel okay about "talking shop" for hours while women listen, but women seem able to talk in men's presence for only a short time before feeling anxious, apologizing, and encouraging the men to speak. If you start to feel wrongly uncomfortable about making males listen, try this exercise: *Keep on talking,* and encourage your sisters to do the same. Honor men by treating them as honestly as you treat women. You will be allowing them to learn.[13]

This is both refreshing and reassuring. That Gloria Steinem uses the phrase "Honor men . . . " and that honoring them consists in assuming the best about them should prove to men and women who do not read *Ms.* magazine that its editor can be trusted. There is no strident polarizing of the sexes evident here but the reverse. It is apparent that she wants women's values to be appreciated and internalized.

In the same chapter, "Men and Women Talking," she explodes three popular myths that have hindered women (and men, too) from relaxed conversation:

(1) Women talk about themselves, personalize, and gossip more than men do. (2) Men would rather talk to men than to mixed groups, and women prefer mixed groups to all-female ones. (3) Women speakers and women's issues are hampered by the feminine style of their presentation.[14]

Women who believe (1)–(3) might well hesitate to open their mouths, and men might think women should do just that (keep their mouths shut). Steinem disabuses them on these three stereotypes. The first two are demonstrably in error, but (3) is hard for most people to accept as specious. A "feminine style" may not be the real reason that explains why a woman speaker cannot make her point effectively. She may be criticized for the way she speaks simply because she's a woman. Or what she is saying may be so unpalatable that it is rejected regardless of what style she projects. Number (3), then, is a problem that needs study. I have made the point earlier that though women who introduce language change have been subjected to ridicule, women who write in an impeccable style have also been ridiculed if the content of their remarks was unpopular. One doesn't have to use singular *they* or neologisms like "herstory" or "girlcott" to be criticized for one's opinions.

Just so, women can be cut down in political discussion (says Steinem) because their style is "too aggressive/weak/loud/quiet." In effect, the medium is *not* the message; the proper medium does not exist for a female speaker. "It is with such paternalistic criticisms that male politicians often dismiss the serious message of a female colleague, or that husbands turn aside the content of arguments made by their wives."[15] In such circumstances a woman can hardly get her point across no matter what style she adopts, yet these disparate criticisms are *not* leveled against women who support conservative causes.

Steinem's perception here is crucial to an understanding of male criticism of female voices:

There are three anomalies that give away this supposedly "helpful" criticism. First, it is rarely used when a woman's message is not challenging to male power. (How often are women criticized for being too fierce in defense of their families? *How often was Phyllis Schlafly criticized for being too aggressive in her opposition to the Equal Rights Amendment?*) Second, the criticism is rarely accompanied by real support, even when the critic presents himself (or herself) as sympathetic. (*Women political candidates say they often get critiques of their fund-raising techniques instead of cash, even from people who agree with them on issues.)* Finally, almost everyone, regardless of status, feels a right to criticize. *(Women professors report criticism of their teaching style from young students, as do women bosses from their employees.)*[16]

Style, then, is often a smokescreen that veils a lack of respect, if not contempt, for women. Women are still subordinate, second-class, and lacking in authority simply by being female. This does not prove that style is irrelevant to women's issues; it means that women must persist in their beliefs despite the negative impression they seem to make when presenting their ideas. It also means that women may retain speech characteristics labeled "feminine" as well as developing new ones that need not strike the hearer or reader as "masculine." Lakoff's "women's language" was ultimately accepted as reality, but the time is now ripe to re-examine her nine traits to see whether they do not contain more positive qualities than the author herself acknowledged.

Many scholars have undertaken this sort of qualitative reappraisal.[17] One example is Virginia Valian's "Linguistics and Feminism."[18] In the first part of her article, Valian scrutinizes Lakoff's pronouncements with regard to adjectives, and she concludes, "In almost all of her comparisons between men's and women's usage, Lakoff assumes that the women's usage is somehow inferior. That assumption seems unwarranted."[19] Valian offers one exception to this generalization: "in her discussion of women's tendency to speak indirectly, where she suggests that both direct and indirect styles of talking are of value."[20]

Adjectives are discussed under two of Lakoff's traits: (1) the "large stock of words related to their specific interests . . . magenta, shirr, dart (in sewing). . . . If men use these words at all, it tends to be tongue-in-cheek" and (2) " 'Empty' adjectives like *divine, charming, cute.* . . ."[21] "Magenta" in (1) and all "empty" adjectives in (2) have a negative connotation—magenta as well as the verb and the noun in (1) because men use them tongue in cheek if at all; "empty" adjectives, by definition. On second thought, why should we care whether technical words such as those in (1) are not used by men or if so, only with a male smirk? Valian suggests that making finer color distinctions is an asset. "If a color is mauve or ecru or crimson, being able to say so is an advantage rather than a liability: there are more true statements that can be made with such a vocabulary than without it. *There is nothing trivial about this ability.*"[22]

With respect to (2) "empty" adjectives, Valian does not use this term, which is in Lakoff's summary of "women's language" traits in Part II of her book. Instead, Valian refers to Part I, where Lakoff says women use more "women's adjectives" (a tautology), whereas men use "neutral" adjectives. "Women's adjectives" overlap with what are called "empty" adjectives in Part II, such as "lovely," "adorable," and "divine." "Neutral" adjectives include "terrific" and "great." I would say that both "women's" and "neutral" adjectives, on the basis of these examples, are to some extent "empty," in the sense of being over-worked, trite, and imprecise or weak in their descriptive power. Valian takes a different tack, pointing out that Lakoff here confuses two issues: (1) which adjectives can appropriately modify which nouns, re-gardless of the speaker's sex, and (2) which adjectives "speakers com-monly use as a function of their sex."[23] Lakoff contends that a woman can say, "What a lovely steel mill," whereas a man cannot. Valian ar-gues that *neither* sex should utter this sentence, for "lovely" (an es-thetic judgment of approval) can scarcely characterize a steel mill.[24] "[I]s the unacceptability to be interpreted not relative to the sentence, but relative to the speaker?" This is one possible conclusion, but Val-ian assumes Lakoff means something slightly different. "That is, the use of such adjectives automatically connotes triviality, and women will use them only if they are willing to be trivial."[25] "Lovely" and the like are still speaker-dependent (rather than context-dependent), but the responsibility for choosing to use the wrong adjective becomes the choice of the woman who is willing (or even prefers) to be trivial. Valian would replace "an image of women as trivia-mongers and sub-stitute an image in which *women are more precise and have larger vocab-ularies than men.*"[26]

Lakoff's judgment of precise adjectives describing color (together with technical nouns like "dart" and verbs like "shirr") appears biased. These lexical items may be the province of women, but that is no rea-son to consider them trivial or silly. If men do not control this vocabu-lary or utter such words only jokingly, the words themselves are not thereby devalued. Suppose, by analogy, that most women do not know a "differential" from a "rocker arm" and only uttered such words with a smirk in the presence of auto mechanics. The mechanics would assume that the women were ignorant; they would not be embarrassed to use these terms in a discussion of automobiles. Therefore, the so-called "trivial" nature of words used by women depends not on the words but on the perception of women's traditional pursuits (sewing, cooking, and other domestic tasks) as trivial.

Can we say the same for other features of "women's language" as described by Lakoff? Number (3), "question intonation," can also be judged on its merits. In Lakoff's classic example where the husband asks when dinner will be ready and the wife replies "Six o'clock?" she can be seen as asking, in effect, if that is a convenient time. Assume for a moment that the husband may have an evening meeting and the children have post-supper activities as well but that the wife's evening is open. "Six o'clock?" is not necessarily a weak and spineless reply. It may be a form of polite consultation. Her answer is necessarily weak only if it forms a habitual pattern, where her time is seen as unimportant by husband and children, in short, where there is no reciprocity. Should she have something scheduled for evening, then she should be able to serve dinner at an hour convenient to herself, and under optimum conditions husband and/or children would take turns making dinner and washing up so that mother can study for the bar exam or read a novel. Question intonation, then, need not be a negative trait but a way of eliciting information and showing consideration for all family members including the wife-mother. If this trait has traditionally been part of "women's language," it could be picked up by husband and children rather than being scrapped as simply "weak" and "powerless."

Gloria Steinem, who feels strongly that women's speech style has much to offer men, quotes Phil Donahue on the tendency of men to converse aggressively, to brag and speechify rather than to engage in a meaningful give and take of ideas:

> "If you're in a social situation, and women are talking to each other, and one woman says, 'I was hit by a car today,' all the other women will say, 'You're kidding! What happened? Where? Are you all right?' In the same situation with males, one male says, 'I was hit by a car today.' I guarantee you there will be another male in the group who will say, 'Wait till I tell you what happened to *me*.' "[27]

It is not surprising that Donahue prefers female audiences if men typically behave in such a boorish fashion. With a male audience he would have a "boast show" rather than a "talk show," and no significant exchange of ideas would take place. Donahue's program would have little educational value, and the portrait he paints of an all-male gathering demonstrates that men's style, not women's, is in need of reform.

If men's "Can you top this?" posture derives from the Big Hunt and is a holdover of prehistoric male "bonding," I pray that it is not in their genes. I assume that bragging, interrupting, and not listening are simply bad habits amenable to change, for not all men are boors, whereas some women are. Steinem urges women to persist in talking, to "honor" men by assuming that the core of their humanity can be reached if women speak up and force them to listen. A hostess needn't let fears overpower her when women continue to talk after the two-minute warning while men ramble on into overtime.

Although Steinem criticizes Lakoff, I see some support for Lakoff's position here. Why would the hostess have to calm her nerves and fortify her resolve to let women have their say if men did not dominate the conversation in social situations? Only a "lady" would be this sensitive. The difference between Steinem and Lakoff is that Lakoff thought men weren't listening because of the way women talked. If they were less tentative, they would gain a more receptive male audience. Steinem's nervous hostess shows that the weak position of women in mixed company is a cultural fact. The hostess was a good deal more nervous in the early to mid-seventies. The issue obviously devolves upon gaining male attention: Steinem's contention is that men typically dominate the conversational arena and will resist letting women have the floor no matter how intelligent they are and no matter what style of speech they adopt. You therefore have to hit the mule over the head with a two-by-four in order to get his attention before you can proceed to train him. Use whatever nouns, adjectives, and verbs you wish: the main thing is to *persist*. That implies relinquishing one's normally polite demeanor, and "polite" in Lakoff's book means the use of excessive reticence, apologies, and hedges. I therefore find some common ground here between the two. Steinem may be more useful at dinner parties; Lakoff, on the job, where assertiveness may result in dismissal.

Lakoff's other "women's language" features (4–9) include "hedges," "so" instead of "very," "hypercorrect grammar" (in which she includes avoidance of "ain't" and "rough language), "superpolite forms" (euphemisms, for example), lack of joke-telling, and "italics" (too frequent vocal stress). All of these can safely be dropped by women in the work place with the exception of (7) "superpolite forms," for in addition to "euphemisms," Lakoff says, "more positively, women are the repositories of tact and know the right things to say to other people, while men carelessly blurt out whatever they are thinking."[28] I cannot see tact as anything but an asset and a quality that is admirable in both men and women.

What about the other traits? Should any of them be preserved on the grounds that they can be construed positively, as Virginia Valian transformed color adjectives? Hedges (4) can be subdivided, for Lakoff first lists "well," "y'know," "kinda," and "sorta"; later in the paragraph she says "another manifestation of the same thing" is "I guess" and similar constructions ("I think," "I wonder"). It is important to recognize that Lakoff admits that *all of these hedges have their uses:* the first group, in situations where one is genuinely uncertain and a hedge represents the most accurate statement of the facts; the latter, "when one has legitimate need for protection, or for deference (if we are afraid that by making a certain statement we are overstepping our rights)," and immediately following, she says that hedges are only a liability *if used to excess.*[29]

The use of "so"—a "weasel word," Lakoff's No. 5—does not strike me as being of the same order of magnitude as the other features. I believe women do use it more than men, but especially young women, say junior high school through freshman year in college where gushy phrases still abound ("he's *so* cute, Jane!"). On a freshman composition I would write a comment in the margin beside "Mary Wollstonecraft was so brave." I would say something like "M.W. was so brave *that what?*" The idea is incomplete. Substituting "very" does not convey a great deal more meaning than "so" in this context, and grammatically "so" calls for a complementary noun clause. But Lakoff is discussing speech, not freshman themes. "So" is rightly called a "weasel word." It might have been subsumed under "hedges" rather than featured as a separate item.

(6) "Hypercorrect grammar. . . . " I think Lakoff has used this term erroneously. "Hypercorrect grammar" means using the *wrong* word because of a misunderstanding of grammatical rules. For example, "John came with she and I." The preposition "with" should be followed by the objective case, "her and me." The origin of this error is

in the objective case being used where the nominative is called for: "Her and me went to the movies." When English teachers and grammar books drill students to use "she and I" as the subject, some students in an excess of zeal avoid "her and me" not only in subject position but everywhere else. Another example of hypercorrection comes from the old radio show Henry Aldridge: "Are you calling I, mother?" Again, an extension of the nominative form where objective is called for. In the predicate nominative position, there has been a longstanding scholary debate over which is correct—"It is I" or "It is me." The former, though technically correct, sounds stilted. For some reason, "This is she" (when you answer the phone and the caller is asking for you but doesn't know your voice) sounds better than "This is her." (When in linguistic binds like this, I usually cop out and say "Speaking.")

Let us ignore Lakoff's label, and look at the content of (6), which covers avoidance of "ain't" and "rough talk," as well as preservation of the suffix "-ing" where boys say "-in." Boys are not scolded for any of these flaws; girls are, because they are "bearers of culture and literacy." "Ain't" seems to be tied into socio-economic status more than to sex, but let us suppose that boys really do escape criticism when they use it as well as "rough language," which I take to include obscenities and swear words (Lakoff gives no examples). "Girls are not supposed to talk rough," she says with respect to (6), and she does not recommend that they should. No. 6 gives the author an opportunity to expose the double standard without obliging her to urge that girls be allowed to follow the boys. In any case, one hears a great many more four-letter words from middle-class females of all ages these days as compared with, say, the early seventies. Women who act like perfect ladies insofar as courtesy and politeness are concerned can routinely be heard to say, "Oh, shit," "So-and-so is an asshole," and even "What the fuck." Such phrases are now so widespread, I cannot attribute their use to a desire to shock. Some women refrain from such "rough language" in public and/or in mixed company; some do not. The double standard in language seems to have been breached. Perhaps women are tired of being everlasting goody-goods.

Let us move on to (7), "superpolite forms." This is the feature for whose retention the best case can be made if one can separate it from (6), for Lakoff says here: "women don't use off-color or indelicate expressions. . . . " Are these words euphemisms for obscene or blasphemous phrases? If so, I have already commented on them in connection with (6), but (7) also calls women "the repositories of tact," and I cannot see how tact can be construed as anything but a virtue. From a verb in Latin meaning "to touch" (*tangere;* past participle *tactus,* whence the substantive), tact is defined as "The ability to appreciate the delicacy of a situation and to do or say the kindest or most fitting thing; diplomacy."[30] Tact is a humane quality applied with intelligence so as to cause as little pain or embarrassment to others as possible. Often, choosing the right words makes the difference between a tactful and a tactless situation. If women possess this combination of good will and finely tuned sensibility to a greater degree than men, they ought to hang on to it. That there are tactless women and tactful men goes without saying, but if Lakoff is right in counting tact among the features of "women's language," then "women's language" ought not to be discarded as "powerless."

I have already commented on (8), "Women don't tell jokes." Women do, but I would prefer to relabel this feature "humor," which many women have in abundance. It is not necessary to be a stand-up comic (Stephanie Brush's "Two flamingos walk into a bar . . . " comes to mind here). Humor is a far more important quality and affects one's dealings with other people of both sexes, of all ages, at home and at work. If Lakoff meant to confine (8) to joke-telling, then she is perhaps correct in saying that women don't generally excel in this area (with some notable exceptions like Joan Rivers and Phyllis Diller), but then all men are not adept at joke-telling either, though they may frequently indulge in it and often in a competitive manner. Since many jokes are at women's expense, women are at least becoming more skilled in parrying such "jokes," a demonstration that they "get" them all right. Many of my women students are excellent joke tellers; what I have noticed recently is that they confess to laughing at chauvinist jokes, jokes that would have offended them five or more years ago. I take this to be a healthy sign; chauvinism has become laughable in its more blatant forms, whereas feminism as a philosophical view of women's potential is moving forward despite the defeat of the Equal Rights Amendment. I see the ability to laugh at chauvinist jokes as a symptom of a somewhat dated disease. The internalization and acceptance of feminist principles makes chauvinist remarks quaint and innocuous. Real sexism or misogyny is another matter and one that does not deserve laughter or even toleration.

Lakoff's last feature of "women's language," (9) "Women speak in italics" is a paradox. It seems forceful to accent words with stress, but the need to strengthen one's speech in this way is viewed as a sign of weakness. I have heard this trait and variations on it such as repetition and asking questions, all of which beg for the attention and approval of the hearer. Gloria Steinem says women must *persist* in speaking without reliance on emphatic stress, repetition, or self-interruption to accomplish the task. Lakoff's position is that dropping trait No. 9 along with 1–8 will aid women's chances of winning recognition from men. Steinem comments along these lines (but without naming Lakoff): "Men *would* support us, we are told, if only we learned how to ask for their support in the right way. It's a subtle and effective way of blaming the victim."[31]

Both Lakoff and Steinem recognize that men have power while women do not. How, then, as a member of a powerless group do we gain men's attention? Steinem presents the following analysis of the problem:

> the less powerful group usually knows the powerful one much better than vice-versa—blacks have had to understand whites in order to survive, women have had to know men—yet the powerful group can afford to regard the less powerful as a mystery. Indeed, the idea of differentness and the Mysterious Other may be necessary justifications for the power imbalance and the lack of sympathy it requires.
>
> One result is that, even when the powerful group *wants* to listen, the other may despair of talking; it's just too much trouble to explain.[32]

Steinem suggests ways to enlighten and inform the powerful group. This one involves speech style: "On issues of style, role reversals are enlightening. For instance, ask a man who is critical of 'aggressive' women to try to argue a serious point while speaking 'like a lady.'" Another ploy is for a woman political candidate to request that men compose a speech in the style they think she should use. I presume the point here is that the exercise puts the burden on men to suggest an appropriate style instead of criticizing whatever style a woman chooses. Another technique is to respond in kind:

> There's a certain satisfaction to saying, in the middle of a man's impassioned speech: "I suppose you have a point to make, but you're not expressing it well. Now, if you just used more personal examples. If you changed your language, your timing, and perhaps your suit. . . ."[33]

Steinem's attitude toward style in language is that women should shed "geisha-like" tones, Marilyn Monroe-like breathy whispers, and other affectations employed by female impersonators. All of these styles derive from trying to please men sexually, to flatter their egos, and to remain in the "safe" but stifling role of worshiper. Women are fortunate in being able to speak in both high and low registers, whereas men restrict their tone of voice to the lower ones (a "manly" voice). Women are free to express more emotions than men through facial expression and body language as well as chattiness. Men, if hampered by the dominant cultural stereotype of the WASP, must demonstrate self-control and therefore censor their emotional responses by taking refuge in silence and a grim visage. Therefore, it behooves women to retain their greater range of expression rather than curbing it.

> A feminist assault on the politics of talking, and listening, is a radical act. It's a way of transforming the cultural vessel in which both instant communication and long-term anthropological change are carried. Unlike the written word, or visual imagery, or any form of communication divorced from our presence, talking and listening won't allow us to hide. There is no neutral page, image, sound, or even a genderless name to protect us. We are demanding to be accepted and understood by all the senses for our whole selves.[34]

There are a number of fundamental ideas in this paragraph: first, that language is a tool of women's liberation; second, that language goes hand in hand with social change. If one were to graph Steinem's implicit view of language and social change, one could not draw it in linear fashion with either language or social change taking chronological first position. A double helix might capture the notion that I derive from Steinem's argument in "Men and Women Talking." Third, language is more than a tool: it's part of culture. It therefore reflects people's changing perceptions as well as functioning as a tool in the process of changing those very perceptions. Fourth, language is never neutral; it is always imbued with some meaning. Therefore, lack of change is as political a stance as changing one's speech and style. Fifth, speech as opposed to writing affords less protection for the individual woman, yet verbal interaction is the prime arena of change.

This is the most succinct outline for the role of language in the cause of feminism I have ever read by a journalist. Steinem has a handle on the experimental nature of human conversation. It takes both optimism about people's underlying good will and courage to persist in spite of rejection and defeat, yet she seems to find the enterprise not only necessary but exhilarating. Her view of language as both a tool of communication and a part of culture is in line with that of the most profound philosophers, psychologists, and linguists, yet many of their articles and books are not readily accessible to the public.* Steinem's paragraph is clear, nontechnical, and audacious. Her advice is sound as well as realistic. She recognizes the possibility— indeed the inevitability—of obstacles, criticisms, and slurs; she promises no quick and easy victory. The demand by women to be understood and accepted for what they are *as they are* is a tall order. "That's precisely," says Steinem, "what makes the change so difficult. And so crucial." She wrote this in 1981, and nothing that has happened in the intervening years makes her observations less relevant today.

In the next decade we may see a breakthrough for women speakers —not just those in the political limelight but women in any work situation and, most important, women in the home. If they persist in seeking to gain men's attention because they have something worthwhile to say rather than to assure themselves of male approval through subservience and a worshipful attitude, the decade 1975–1984 may seem in retrospect as old-fashioned as a daguerrotype. Let us hope so.

In the mean time, perhaps the following aphorisms will provide cause for optimism:

The Wish is Father to the Thought
but
Necessity is the Mother of Invention.

* Steinem's sources can be found in her article "The Politics of Talking in Groups: How to Win the Game *and* Change the Rules" (*Ms.*, May, 1981, pp. 43ff.). At the end ("For Further Reading") she lists a dozen prominent linguists, including Nancy Henley, Cheris Kramarae, Dale Spender, Sally McConnell-Ginet, Nelly Furman, Ruth Borker, and Wendy Martyna. Other scholars are mentioned in the body of the article, which was shortened considerably for *Outrageous Acts and Everyday Rebellions.*

Afterword

The study of women and language is being pursued by scholars in a variety of fields in addition to linguistics, as the references in the preceding pages show. Philosophers, psychologists, sociologists, editors, lexicographers, journalists, anthropologists, and English teachers have all made significant contributions to the field. The interdisciplinary nature of this endeavor is striking: language can be studied in a vacuum but not language, women, and society. This fact is demonstrated by Robin Lakoff's departure from transformational generative grammar to sociolinguistics. After *Language and Woman's Place*, Lakoff published some articles on language and sex, but most recently she has gone into semiotics, a field that both comprehends and transcends linguistics. Semiotics (the science of signs and symbols) includes nonverbal as well as linguistic transactions. At its most dense and difficult it analyzes theories of codes and sign production. If you thought *The Name of the Rose* was a challenge, try reading Umberto Eco's earlier work *A Theory of Semiotics* (Bloomington: Indiana University Press, 1976). If you're a Walker Percy fan *(The Moviegoer, The Last Gentleman, Love in the Ruins)*, browse through *The Message in the Bottle: How Queer Man Is, How Queer Language Is, and What One Has to Do with the Other* (New York: Farrar Straus and Giroux, 1975), especially chapter 11, "Semiotic and a Theory of Knowledge."

Semiotics, however, is also the study of signs in the market place—the area of popular culture. I remember auditing a course in esthetics at the Sorbonne in which the professor showed slides of cheese boxes labelled "La Vache Qui Rit" and those of a rival company, "La Vache

140

Sérieuse" ("The Laughing Cow" vs. "The Serious Cow"), now available in your local supermarket. I was entranced at the witty and learned way the eminent philosopher analyzed everyday household items for overt and hidden meanings in the pictures, so entranced that I considered changing my major from French to philosophy. However, when I returned to Duke University for my senior year, I found no comparable faculty member and hence remained a language major, ultimately embarking upon a Ph.D. in Indo-European Linguistics—a fascinating field but one that immersed me in the study of ancient languages, a far cry from anything so "frivolous" as cheese box labels. However, once minted in 1967, I was drawn back to the study of communication systems besides language. When I taught a course called "Nonverbal Communication" for the Anthropology Department at the University of Colorado, I entered a field that considered pictures as important as words, and body language, flags, insignia, and silent movies as worthy of study as the Sanskrit verb system. I ultimately published two articles in the journal *Semiotica*, one dealing with the cartoons of the 1976 Carter presidential campaign and the other on Hitler's swastika flag.

It therefore did not come as a total shock to me when Robin Tolmach Lakoff ventured into the area of semiotics and popular culture with the publication of *Face Value: The Politics of Beauty* (London: Routledge & Kegan Paul, 1984), coauthored with Raquel L. Scherr. This engrossing book on the perception of female beauty and how this concept affects women may prove to be another "goad" (like *Language and Woman's Place*) especially to those academic and intellectual women who disdain personal looks as a topic worth studying. *Face Value* should be compared with Betty Friedan's *The Feminine Mystique* (1963) for its confrontation with a taboo subject. Beauty is not a "problem that has no name" but a problem that is not viewed as a problem by many feminists:

> Maybe with close friends, as we had become over two years of team-teaching, the thoughts too private for words could be given a voice, but always, up till that moment, as defining your individual neurosis, your secret shame. We had spent time, of course, in consciousness-raising groups in earlier years, and in them we had thought we had dealt with *every* woman's secret, every hidden shame, desire, fear, hope . . . and yet the subject had never to our recollection been mentioned, not in those groups of thoughtful, feminist, politically-savvy and angry women. That in itself was curious, we were eventually to realize, but not yet. At first it

was just with a personal sense of relief that we realized that there were
words for it, that someone else had thought the same thoughts, felt the
same anguish, hope, fear, fury—and never spoken of it to another soul.
(p. 14)

By contrast with Lakoff, Cheris Kramarae, who received her Ph.D.
in Speech Communication in 1975, has continued publishing on
women and language so that she now has to her credit a sizeable number of important articles, books, and papers presented at scholarly
meetings. *Women and Language News* has moved from Stanford to the
University of Illinois under her aegis and that of Paula A. Treichler.
Kramarae and Treichler have also collaborated on *A Feminist Dictionary* (London: Routledge & Kegan Paul, 1985), an illustrated reference book whose purpose is to pull together

> the divers literature on language and gender . . . ; identify the issues of
> language theory, practice, and policy feminists have raised, now and in
> the past; show the ways in which women are "seizing the language"; and
> illustrate the words and other forms of expression (tapestries, cartoons,
> photographs) women use to conceptualize, reflect upon, and describe the
> world.

The four-page brochure (from which I have quoted) includes photo-
graphs, lampoons, symbols, and comic strips plus a partial list of entries, demonstrating that the dictionary will be useful to a wide range
of readers, including those interested in semiotics and popular culture.

Marie Shear has written an excellent survey of nonsexist usage—
"Equal Writes," *The Women's Review of Books*, I, No. 11 (August, 1984),
12–13. She lists close to fifty sources and especially recommends *Words
and Women: New Language in New Times* by Casey Miller and Kate Swift
(Garden City, N.Y.: Anchor, 1977), the book attacked so viciously by
John Simon apparently because the jacket cover revealed that the authors resembled neither Brooke Shields nor Cheryl Tiegs.

> The broadest, liveliest survey of sexist usage—how it works, where it's
> found, and why it matters—is *Words and Women*. . . . This contemporary
> classic explains the origins, pervasiveness, and perniciousness of such us-
> age in more depth than handbooks have room for, and it's written in
> English, not Scholarspeak. Whatever handbooks you pick to cover the
> mechanics, pick *Words and Women* to cover meaning.

In Shear's opinion very few of the features of sexist language raised ten or more years ago have ceased to exist. Perhaps we will have to spend another decade preaching to the unconverted, for the ways in which language discriminates against women are tenaciously ingrained.

It is encouraging that what could have been a minor subdivision of linguistics has blossomed into a vigorous garden with roots in many academic disciplines as well as in popular culture. Should women and language have remained the province of linguists only, I shudder to think how little impact the subject would have had by now, for linguistics is largely a mystery to the general public. Fortunately, women in ever greater numbers are "seizing the language," as Cheris Kramarae and Paula Treichler so aptly state, and it is high time.

Notes

Introduction

1. "Father Time," *Studies in Iconology: Humanistic Themes in the Art of the Renaissance* (New York: Harper Torchbooks, 1962), pp. 69–93. The Bowery Savings Bank cartoon is found on p. 69.

2. Muriel Gardiner, ed. *The Wolf-Man. With the Case of the Wolf-Man* (Nev York: Basic Books, 1971).

3. Erich Fromm, *Greatness and Limitations of Freud's Thought* (New York: Harper, 1980), pp. 7–8, 15–16.

4. Ibid., p. 16.

5. Warren Farrell proposed *te* for *he* or *she*, *tes* for *his* or *her*, and *tir* for *him* or *her* in *The Liberated Man: Beyond Masculinity: Freeing Men and Their Relationships with Women* (New York: Bantam, 1975). "Herstory" has cropped up everywhere and was used as a book title by June Sochen, with the subtitle *A Record of the American Woman's Past* (Sherman Oaks, Calif.; Alfred Publishing Co., Inc., 1981).

6. Spender, *Women of Ideas*, p. 2.

1. Women's Language

1. Robin Lakoff, *Language and Woman's Place* (New York: Colophon Books, 1975). Pages 1–50 are a reprint of an article of the same name published in the sociolinguistic journal *Language in Society*, 2 (1973), 45–79. Part II (pp. 51–83) entitled "Why Women Are Ladies," appeared in Volume I of Charles Fillmore, George Lakoff, and Robin Lakoff, eds., *Berkeley Studies in Syntax and Semantics* (Berkeley: University of California Press, 1974). Lakoff also wrote "You Are What You Say," *Ms.* (July, 1974), pp. 65–67.

2. Lakoff, *Language and Woman's Place*, pp. 4, 5. Hereinafter cited as *LAWP*.

3. "Women and Politeness: A New Perspective on Language and Society," *Reviews in Anthropology* (May/June, 1976), pp. 240–49. Citation from p. 240.

4. *Signs: Journal of Women in Culture and Society*, 1 (1976), 744.

5. "Breaking the Double Binds," *Language and Style*, 13 (Fall, 1980), 81–93. Citation from pp. 81–82.

6. Ibid., p. 84.

7. "Women's Language in America: Myth and Reality," in *Women's Language and Style*, ed. Douglas Butturff and Edmund L. Epstein (Akron, Ohio: L

& S Books, 1978), pp. 47–61. Quotation from p. 54. On the same page Frank compares Lakoff to Otto Jespersen, who included a chapter on women in *Language: Its Nature, Development and Origin,* published in 1922. The similarity between the two is in their "lack of empirical evidence"—not surprising to Frank in the case of Jespersen given the early date of his book but quite surprising in the case of Lakoff. (See also Frank, pp. 47–48.) Otto Jespersen's work—virtually the first that discussed women's language at all—cannot conveniently be reviewed within the limits of this book, and so I am treating him and his influence on later linguists in an article called "Jespersen's Ghost."

8. Frank, "Women's Language in America," p. 54.

9. Ibid. (My italics.)

10. See, for example, Betty Lou Dubois and Isabel Crouch, "The Question of Tag Questions in Women's Speech: They Don't Really Use More of Them, Do They?" *Language in Society,* 4 (1975), 289–94.

11. *Man Made Language* (London: Routledge & Kegan Paul, 1980), pp. 46–47.

12. Spender, *Man Made Language,* p. 47.

13. *LAWP,* p. vii.

14. Mary Ritchie Key, *Male/Female Language* (Metuchen, N.J.: Scarecrow Press, 1975) grew out of Key's pioneering course on language and women. Key may have been the first to offer a course on the subject. See p. v. Barrie Thorne and Nancy Henley, eds., *Language and Sex* (Rowley, Mass.: Newbury House, 1975) forms part of the "Series in Sociolinguistics" edited by Roger W. Shuy of Georgetown University and the Center for Applied Linguistics.

15. Noam Chomsky, *Syntactic Structures* (The Hague: Mouton & Co., 1957).

16. Cheris Kramer, "Folk-linguistics: Wishy-Washy Mommy Talk," *Psychology Today,* June, 1984, pp. 82–85. Lakoff is mentioned on p. 84.

17. Ibid., p. 83.

18. *LAWP,* p. 59.

19. Ibid., p. 58.

20. Ibid.

21. Kramer, "Folk-linguistics . . . ," p. 85.

22. *LAWP,* p. 59.

23. Ibid., p. 51.

24. Ibid., pp. 51–52.

25. Ibid., p. 52.

26. Ibid., p. 53.

27. Ibid., pp. 53–56.

28. Ibid., pp. 60–61.

29. Gregory Bateson, *Steps to an Ecology of Mind,* Part III: "Form and Pathology in Relationship" (New York: Ballantine, 1972). Cited by Lakoff on p. 61 and in the bibliography, unnumbered p. 85.

30. Horner's work on achievement motivation in women can be found in popular form in "Fail: Bright Women," *Psychology Today,* November, 1969, pp. 36–38, 62. Both Horner and Lakoff came under fire for presenting what were at the time unpalatable ideas, but the criticisms seem not to have thwarted their careers. Lakoff was promoted to full professor at Berkeley in 1976, the year after her controversial book was published. Horner was named President of Radcliffe in 1972 at the age of 32, the youngest person to achieve that office since the founding of the college.

31. Ibid., p. 38.

32. Ibid.

33. Ibid. (My italics.)

34. Ibid., p. 36.

35. Psychologists have largely dismissed Horner's work, having failed to replicate her results. Despite the statistical argument, I have retained the "stories" that students wrote for Horner at the University of Michigan. Such individual accounts do not fall under the "replication" edict but reflect a piece of history and are valid simply as personal observations.

36. *LAWP*, p. 73.

37. Ibid., p. 45.

38. Ibid., p. 46.

39. Ibid., p. 36.

40. Ibid., p. 42.'

2. Crossing the Dialect Frontier

1. Betty Friedan, *The Feminine Mystique* (New York: Dell, 1970; reprint of W. W. Norton edition of 1963), pp. 11–27. Friedan composed her book between June 1957 and July 1962, though she had spent far longer collecting the data.

2. Ibid., p. 15. The first time that Friedan heard a housewife mention "the problem" was in April, 1959. This reference was immediately recognized and discussed by the others present so that they left the Kaffeeklatsch with a sense of relief.

3. John Skow, "Erma in Bomburbia," *Time*, July 2, 1984, p. 64. Cover article. The picture of a smiling Bombeck is captioned "HOW ERMA COPES: Working the House for Laughs." Three quotes reveal not only her sense of humor but also her perception that "the happy housewife" image was indeed a myth: "Housework, if you do it right, can kill you." "Why take pride in cooking, when they don't take pride in eating?" and "Guilt is the gift that keeps on giving."

4. Friedan, *Feminine Mystique*, p. 50.

5. Betty Friedan, *The Second Stage* (New York: Summit Books, 1981), p. 27.

6. First published in 1956 as *Die Dämonen* on the anniversary of Doderer's sixtieth birthday. English translation by Richard and Clara Winston (New York: Alfred A. Knopf, 1961).

7. Doderer, *Demons*, p. 536.

8. Ibid., pp. 536–37.

9. Ibid., p. 539.

10. Ibid.

11. Ibid., p. 540.

12. Ibid., pp. 564–65.

13. Ibid., p. 1291.

14. Ibid., p. 1293.

15. Friedan, *Feminine Mystique*, p. 144.

16. Ibid., p. 148.

17. Phyllis McGinley, *Sixpence in Her Shoe* (New York: Macmillan, 1964), p. 47.

18. Ibid.

19. This marvelous phrase was invented by Annette Kolodny. See "Honing a Habitable Languagescape: Women's Images for the New World Frontiers," in *Women and Language in Literature and Society*, ed. Sally McConnell-Ginet, Ruth Borker, and Nelly Furman (New York: Praeger, 1980), pp. 188–204.

20. Bernard Shaw, *Androcles and the Lion, Overruled, Pygmalion* (New York: Brentano's, 1916).

21. Shaw, *Pygmalion,* pp. 109–112.

22. Ibid., p. 197.

23. Ibid., p. 203.

24. Ibid., p. 209.

25. Dick Francis, *For Kicks* (New York: Pocket Books, 1974; reprint of the Harper & Row edition of 1965), p. 31.

26. Ibid., pp. 31–32.

3. Linguists and Laypeople

1. *Webster's New International Dictionary of the English Language,* Second Edition, Unabridged, ed. William Allan Neilson et al. (Springfield, Mass.: G. & C. Merriam Company, 1946). The third edition under the editorship of Philip Babcock Gove first appeared in 1961.

2. Geoffrey Nunberg, "The Decline of Grammar," *The Atlantic Monthly,* December, 1983, p. 34.

3. See "The Making of a Nonsexist Dictionary," in *Language and Sex: Difference and Dominance,* ed. Barrie Thorne and Nancy Henley (Rowley, Mass.: Newbury House, 1975), pp. 57–63 (reprinted from *Ms.* magazine, Dec., 1973, pp. 12–14, 16). Graham says that *The American Heritage School Dictionary,* begun in 1969 and published in 1972, was the first dictionary to recognize "Ms." She was Executive Editor of American Heritage Publishing Company's Dictionary Division at the time.

4. Graham, "The Making . . . ," p. 60. Actually, Graham wrote the definition, and gives credit to Editor-in-Chief Peter Davies for the derivation.

5. Emily Post, *Etiquette: The Blue Book of Social Usage,* 10th ed. (New York: Funk and Wagnalls, 1960), p. 27. The publishing history of this book is illuminating: "Original Edition, Copyright 1922; Revised Editions, Copyright, 1927, 1931, 1934, 1940, 1942, 1945, 1950, and 1955 by Funk & Wagnalls Company. *Ninety-first printing*" (unnumbered p. iv; italics in the original). That the copyright was renewed in the midst of World War II boggles my mind.

6. Ibid., p. 26. (My italics.)

7. Graham, "The Making . . . ," p. 59.

8. Marjorie B. U'Ren, "The Image of Woman in Textbooks," in *Woman in Sexist Society: Studies in Power and Powerlessness,* eds. Vivian Gornick and Barbara K. Moran (New York: New American Library, 1972; reprint of hardback edition by Basic Books, 1971), pp. 318–328. Quotation from p. 322. (My italics.)

9. Ibid., p. 323.

10. Ibid., p. 321.

11. Ibid., p. 323.

12. Elizabeth Fisher, "Children's Books: The Second Sex, Junior Division," in *And Jill Came Tumbling After,* ed. Judith Stacey, Susan Bereaud, and Joan Daniels (New York: Dell, 1974).

13. Nancy Chodorow, "Being and Doing: A Cross-Cultural Examination of the Socialization of Males and Females," in *Woman in Sexist Society,* eds. Gornick and Moran, pp. 259–291. Quotation from p. 285.

14. Ibid., p. 286.

15. Friedan, *The Feminine Mystique,* p. 344.

16. Ibid., pp. 151–152.

17. Ibid., pp. 152–153.

18. Betty Swords, "McGraw-Hill and Scott, Foresman Take Giant Leap into the Present," *Writer's Digest*, Feb., 1975, pp. 9–10.

19. Ibid., p. 9.

20. "Guidelines for Equal Treatment of the Sexes in McGraw-Hill Book Company Publications" (New York: McGraw-Hill Book Company, n.d.), p. 1.

21. Ibid. (My italics.)

22. Ibid., p. 2

23. Ibid.

24. Ibid., p. 3. (My italics.)

25. George F. Will, "Sexist Guidelines and Reality," *The Washington Post*, Sept. 20, 1974. Reprinted in *The Denver Post* as "Glib Lib Aims at Word Purge," Oct. 1, 1974.

26. Ibid. (Ellipsis in the original.)

27. Ibid.

28. Ibid.

29. Ibid.

30. *The Denver Post*, October 14, 1974, p. 27.

31. Helen B. Andelin, *Fascinating Womanhood* (Clovis, Calif.: Pacific Press, 1965), unnumbered p. 6.

32. William L. O'Neill, *Everyone Was Brave: A History of Feminism in America.* With a New Afterword by the Author. (Chicago: Quandrangle Books, 1971), p. 363. This quotation from the New Afterword cannot be found in reprints of the original hardback edition of 1969.

4. Pronoun Envy

1. "The Language of Religion," in *Words and Women*, eds. Casey Miller anc Kate Swift (Garden City, N.Y.: Doubleday/Anchor, 1976), pp. 75–76.

2. Mary Ritchie Key, *Male/Female Language* (Metuchen, N.J.: Scarecrow Press, 1975), p. 142. The chapter in which the quotation occurs is entitled "An Androgynous Language: The Future Tense." (My italics.)

3. Miller and Swift, *Words and Women*, p. 76.

4. Ibid., p. 55.

5. Ibid., p. 57. Both quotes from Watkins were taken from "Indo-European and the Indo-Europeans," *The American Heritage Dictionary of the English Language* (New York: American Heritage Publishing Company, 1969), p. 1498.

6. Miller and Swift, *Words and Women*, pp. 76–77, quoting Armagost's Let ter to the Editor in *Newsweek*, December 27, 1971.

7. Ann Bodine, "Androcentrism in Prescriptive Grammar: Singular 'They,' Sex-Indefinite 'He,' and "He or She,'" *Language in Society*, 4 (1975), 129–146.

8. Ibid., pp. 130–131.

9. Ibid., p. 131. (My italics.)

10. Ibid., pp. 131–133.

11. Ibid., p. 133.

12. Ibid.

13. Ibid., p. 138.

14. Ibid., p. 139, quoting Paul Roberts, *The Roberts English Series* (New York: Harcourt, Brace and World, 1967), p. 355.

15. Bodine, "Androcentrism," p. 140.

16. Ibid., p. 141. Conklin presented her "perspectives" paper at a meeting of

the American Dialect Society, Ann Arbor, in 1973.

17. James R. Hulbert, ed., *Bright's Anglo-Saxon Reader* (New York: Henry Holt, 1957; original copyright 1891), p. liii.

18. "Guidelines," p. 8.

19. Ibid. It seems to me that *or* should be italicized in the phrase *"he* or *she."*

20. Ibid. (My italics.)

21. For two philosphers' opinions on both generic *he* and the noun *man*, see Janice Moulton, "The Myth of the Neutral 'Man,'" in *Sexist Language: A Modern Philosophical Analysis*, ed. Mary Vetterling-Braggin (n.p.: Littlefield, Adams, 1981), pp. 199–115, and a counter argument by Jane Duran, "Gender-Neutral Terms," ibid., pp. 147–154.

22. Martyna's doctoral dissertation is entitled "Using and Understanding the Generic Masculine: A Social-Psychological Approach to Language and the Sexes" (Ph.D., Stanford 1978), but she had begun publishing before receiving her degree.

23. Wendy Martyna, "Comprehension of the Generic Masculine: Inferring 'She' from 'He,'" paper presented at the American Psychological Association, 85th Annual Convention, San Francisco, California, August, 1977, p. 9. I am indebted to the author for having sent me a copy of this paper in December, 1977.

24. Ibid., p. 9.

25. Ibid., p. 14. (My italics.)

26. Ibid., pp. 14–15.

27. Ibid., p. 16.

28. Ibid., p. 17.

29. Ibid., p. 19.

30. Ibid., quoting and paraphrasing J. P. Stanley, "Gender-marking in American English: Usage and Reference," in *Sexism and Language*, ed. A. P. Nilsen et al. (Urbana: National Council of Teachers of English, 1977).

31. William Strunk, Jr., With Revisions, an Introduction, and a Chapter on Writing by E. B. White, *The Elements of Style*, 3d ed. (New York: Macmillan, 1979), p. 60.

32. Wendy Martyna, "The Psychology of the Generic Masculine," in *Women and Language in Literature and Society*, eds. Sally McConnell-Ginet, Ruth Borker, and Nelly Furman (New York: Praeger, 1980), pp. 69–78. Quotation from p. 75.

33. Martyna, "Psychology," drawing upon Ritchie's article "Alice Through the Statutes," *McGill Law Journal*, 21 (1975), 685–707.

34. Ida Husted Harper, *The Life and Work of Susan B. Anthony* (Indianapolis: Bowen-Merrill, 1898), II, 982.

35. *Webster's New World Dictionary with Student Handbook*, Concise Editior (Nashville, Tenn.: The Southwestern Company, 1975), *Student Handbook*, p. 17. (My italics.)

36. Webster, *Handbook*, p. 25. (My italics.)

37. Ibid., p. 26.

38. Carol Felsenthal, *The Sweetheart of the Silent Majority: The Biography of Phyllis Schlafly* (Garden City, N.Y.: Doubleday, 1981).

39. Simone de Beauvoir, *The Second Sex*, trans. and ed. H. M. Parshley (New York: The Modern Library, 1968), p. xix. Originally published in France in two volumes as *Le Deuxième Sexe* (Librairie Gallimard, 1949).

40. Hunter College Women's Studies Collective, *Women's Realities, Women' Choices* (New York: Oxford University Press, 1983). The eight members of the Collective are identified on pp. v–vi.

41. Collective, *Women's Realities,* pp. x–xi.

42. George F. Will, "Sexist Guidelines and Reality," The Washington *Post,* September 20, 1974; William F. Buckley, Jr., "On the Right: Who's Beautiful?" Middleton (Conn.) *Press,* November 30, 1972; Kanfer's article appeared in *Time,* October 23, 1972, p. 79.

43. Carolyn G. Heilbrun, *Toward a Recognition of Androgyny* (New York: W. W. Norton, 1982; originally published by Alfred A. Knopf, 1964), p. x.

44. Mary Daly, *Beyond God the Father: Toward a Philosophy of Women's Liberation* (Boston: Beacon Press, 1973), pp. 10–11. (My italics) Daly's first book, published in 1968, was entitled *The Church and the Second Sex.*

5. Names and Titles

1. Mary Daly, *Beyond God the Father: Toward a Philosophy of Women's Liberation* (Boston: Beacon Press, 1973), p. 8.

2. Cheris Kramarae, *Women and Men Speaking: Frameworks for Analysis* (Rowley, Mass.: Newbury House, 1981), p. viii. I am grateful to Professor Kramarae for sending me this reference. In her letter she remarked that at least forty of her friends have changed their names and that she herself considers names a very significant topic.

3. Ibid., p. ix.

4. Daly, *Beyond God,* p. 167.

5. Ibid., p. 2.

6. Ibid. (My italics.)

7. Ibid., p. 8.

8. Ibid.

9. For a thoughtful review of *Pure Lust,* see Marilyn Frye, "Famous Lust Words," *The Women's Review of Books,* August, 1984, pp. 3–4.

10. See Sally McConnell-Ginet, Ruth Borker, and Nelly Furman, eds., *Women and Language in Literature and Society* (New York: Praeger, 1980), pp. 174–87. Quotation from p. 181. (My italics)

11. Emily Post, *Etiquette: The Blue Book of Social Usage,* 10th ed. (New York: Funk and Wagnalls, 1960), p. 537.

12. Ibid.

13. Ibid.

14. Michael Levin, "Vs. Ms." in *Sexist Language: A Modern Philosophical Analysis,* ed. Mary Vetterling-Braggin (n.p.: Littlefield, Adams, 1981), p. 217, footnote.

15. Ibid., p. 217.

16. Ibid. (My italics.)

17. Ibid., p. 218.

18. Ibid. "Unsupportable" is not in the dictionary. He means "insupportable."

19. Ibid., p. 218. (My italics.)

20. Ibid., p. 221.

21. Ibid., p. 219.

22. Ibid., pp. 219–220. (My italics.)

23. See István Fodor, "The Origin of Grammatical Gender, I," *Lingua,* 8

(1959), 1–41, and "The Origin of Grammatical Gender, II," *Lingua,* 8 (1959), 186–214.

24. Levin, "Vs. Ms.," p. 220.

25. Ibid., pp. 220–221.

26. Ibid., p. 219.

27. L. M. Purdy, "Against 'Vs. Ms.,' " in *Sexist Language,* ed. Mary Vetterling-Braggin, pp. 223–228. Quoted material from p. 224.

28. Ibid., p. 225.

29. Ibid., pp. 226–227.

30. Alan Soble, "Beyond the Miserable Vision of 'Vs. Ms.,'" in *Sexist Language,* ed. Mary Vetterling-Braggin, pp. 229–248. Quotation from p. 229.

31. Ibid., pp. 234, 235.

32. Ibid., p. 241.

33. Ibid., p. 243.

34. Ibid.

35. Ibid.

36. Ibid.

37. Ibid., pp. 244–245.

38. Ibid., p. 245.

39. Joseph Wambaugh, *The Delta Star* (New York: Bantam/Perigord, 1984; originally published by William Morrow, 1983), p. 193. (Wambaugh's italics)

40. McConnell-Ginet, Borker, and Furman, *Women,* Editors' Introduction, p. xi.

41. William Safire, "On Language" (column title), "Euphemism Vote: Goodbye Sex, Hello Gender," *The Sunday Denver Post, Contemporary,* 12 August 1984, pp. 18, 42 and 44. From *The New York Times.*

42. Safire, "Euphemism Vote," p. 42.

43. Ibid., p. 44.

44. Ibid.

45. Ibid.

6. Terms of Endearment

1. Wolfson and Manes, "Don't 'Dear' Me!" in *Women and Language in Literature and Society,* ed. Sally McConnell-Ginet, Ruth Borker, and Nelly Furman (New York: Praeger, 1980), pp. 79–92.

2. Ibid., p. 80.

3. Ibid., p. 81.

4. Ibid., (My italics.)

5. Ibid., p. 82.

6. Ibid.

7. Ibid. (My italics.)

8. Ibid., p. 84.

9. Ibid., p. 85. (My italics.)

10. Ibid. (My italics.)

11. Ibid., p. 89.

12. Ibid., p. 88.

13. Ibid., p. 89.

14. Ibid., p. 90.

15. Ibid.

16. Ibid., pp. 90, 91.

17. Emma Elliot, "'My Name Is Mrs. Simon,' " *Ladies' Home Journal,* August,

1984, pp. 18, 21, 150.

18. Ibid., p. 150. (My italics.)

19. Ibid.

20. Stephanie Brush, *Men: An Owner's Manual* (New York: Linden Press/ Simon & Schuster, 1984).

21. Cutler Durkee, "Got a Lemon? Stephanie Brush, Author of *Men: An Owner's Manual,* Will Help You Fix Your Fella," *People,* 6 August 1984, p. 90.

22. Ibid.

23. Ibid.

24. Ibid.

25. Fran Lebowitz, "Parental Guidance," *Social Studies* (New York: Pocket Books, 1982), pp. 29–30.

26. Ibid., p. 30.

27. Ibid., p. 31.

28. Ibid., p. 32.

29. Fran Lebowitz, "The Servant Problem," *Social Studies,* pp. 46–47.

30. Ibid., p. 47. (My italics.)

31. Durkee, "Got a Lemon?," p. 90.

32. Ibid.

33. Ibid.

34. Erma Bombeck, "Profile of a Martyress," *If Life Is a Bowl of Cherries-What Am I Doing in the Pits?* (New York: McGraw-Hill, 1978), p. 67, 68–69.

35. Jeff Greenfield, "A Rapier Instead of a Bludgeon," *The Denver Post,* 7 August 1984, p. 14A.

36. Ibid. (My italics.)

37. Ibid.

38. Ibid.

39. Trisha Flynn, "Smile: Women of Different Political Views Identify with Accomplishments of Their Sex," *Contemporary, The Sunday Denver Post,* 12 August 1984, p. 2.

7. The Language Gene

1. Helen Lambert argues that whatever the hereditary characteristics of males and females are (or turn out to be, in the light of new research), matters of social justice should ignore the Nature/Nurture stereotypes. See "Biology and Equality: A Perspective on Sex Differences," *Signs: Journal of Women in Culture and Society,* 4, no. 1 (1978), 97–117.

2. "Sex Differences in Mental and Behavioral Traits, *Genetic Psychology Monographs,* 77 (1968), 169–299.

3. "Sex and Language Acquisition—Is There Any Influence?" *Journal of Pragmatics,* 5 (1981), 1–25.

4. Joanna Russ, *How to Suppress Women's Writing* (Austin: University of Texas Press, 1983). Compare the brilliant much earlier book by Mary Ellmann, *Thinking About Women* (New York: Harcourt Brace Jovanovich, 1968), especially "Differences in Tone," pp. 147–74.

5. Russ, *Suppress,* p. 39.

6. John Simon, *Paradigms Lost,* subtitled *Reflections on Literacy and Its Decline* (New York: Clarkson N. Potter, n.d.).

7. Ibid., 33–38.

8. Ibid., p. 37.

9. That the language of myth is in the imperative is suggested by Elizabeth

Janeway in *Man's World, Woman's Place: A Study in Social Mythology* (New York: William Morrow, 1971), Chapter 3, pp. 37–47.

10. Simon, *Paradigms,* p. x.

11. Ibid.

12. Ibid., p. xi.

13. Ibid., p. 37. The word "androgyny" is italicized by Simon.

14. Ibid., p. 36.

15. Ibid., pp. 37–38. (My italics.)

16. Ibid., p. 38.

17. His defense of "Jewess" and "Negress" can be found, Simon, *Paradigms,* p. 35.

18. Janeway, *Man's World,* pp. 37–38. Janeway assumes that her readers are conversant with "mood" in the English verb system as opposed to "voice"— active/passive. The imperative mood governs commands; the optative, wishes; and the declarative, statements of fact.

19. Ibid., pp. 40–41.

20. *LAWP,* p. 76.

21. Ibid., p. 77.

22. Ibid., pp. 78–79.

23. Ibid., p. 79.

24. Ibid.

25. *New York Times Magazine,* 25 October 1970, pp. 35–37, 124–127, 132, 134, and 136.

26. Tiger, "Male Dominance," p. 136.

27. Sally Slocum, "Woman the Gatherer: Male Bias in Anthropology," *Toward an Anthropology of Women,* ed. Rayna R. Reiter (New York: Monthly Review Press, 1975), pp. 36–50.

28. Ibid., pp. 42–43. (My italics.)

29. *Women and Language in Literature and Society* (New York: Praeger, 1980), Editors' Introduction, p. xi. (My italics.)

30. In McConnell-Ginet et al., *Women and Language,* pp. 93–110.

31. O'Barr and Atkins, "'Powerless Language?'" p. 93.

32. Ibid., p. 95, quoting F. Lee Bailey and Henry B. Rothblatt, *Successful Techniques for Criminal Trials* (Rochester, N.Y.: Lawyers Co-operative Publishing Co., 1971), p. 190.

33. O'Barr and Atkins, "'Powerless Language?'" p. 99 and footnote.

34. Ibid., p. 102. The statement that more women than men use WL features appears on pp. 103–104.

35. Ibid., p. 106.

36. Ibid., p. 107.

37. Ibid., pp. 109–110.

38. *LAWP,* p. 55.

39. O'Barr and Atkins, "'Powerless Language?'" p. 104.

40. O'Barr, *Linguistic Evidence,* p. 62.

41. Ibid., pp. 63–64. (My italics.)

42. Ibid., p. 64.

43. Ibid., p. 67.

8. Futurespeak

1. *LAWP,* p. 51.

2. Ibid., pp. 51–52.

3. Ibid., pp. 74–75.

4. Ibid., p. 75.

5. Ibid., p. 80.

6. Ibid., p. 81.

7. Ibid., p. 83.

8. Ibid.

9. S. J. Phelps (Littleton), "Why Nominate Ferraro?" *The Denver Post,* 22 August 1984, p. 25A.

10. Gloria Steinem, "Men and Women Talking," *Outrageous Acts and Everyday Rebellions* (New York: Holt, Rinehart and Winston, 1983), pp. 176–190. Quotation from p. 180.

11. Ibid., p. 181. (My italics.)

12. Ibid., p. 183.

13. Ibid., p. 181.

14. Ibid., p. 182.

15. Ibid., p. 184.

16. Ibid. (My italics.)

17. See the annotated bibliography in Barrie Thorne, Cheris Kramarae, and Nancy Henley, eds., *Language, Gender, and Society* (Rowley, Mass.: Newbury House, 1983), pp. 151–331.

18. Virginia Valian, "Linguistics and Feminism," *Sexist Language: A Modern Philosophical Analysis,* ed. Mary Vetterling-Braggin (n.p.: Littlefield, Adams, 1981), pp. 68–80.

19. Ibid., p. 71.

20. Ibid., p. 80, note 5.

21. *LAWP,* p. 53.

22. Valian, "Linguistics," p. 69. (My italics.)

23. Ibid.

24. Ibid., p. 70.

25. Ibid.

26. Ibid. (My italics.)

27. Gloria Steinem, "Men and Women," p. 182.

28. *LAWP,* p. 55.

29. Ibid., p. 54.

30. *The American Heritage Dictionary,* Second College Edition (Boston: Houghton Mifflin, 1982), p. 1237.

31. Steinem, "Men and Women," p. 184.

32. Ibid., p. 185.

33. Ibid.

34. Ibid., p. 190.

Index

ALETTE OLIN HILL, associate professor of
English and Women's Studies at Metropolitan
State College, Denver, has published articles in
such prestigious scholarly journals as *Semiotica,*
and *The American Historical Review.*